KNOW IT! PRAY IT! LIVE IT!

A Family Guide to

The Catholic Youth Bible

KNOW IT! PRAY IT! LIVE IT!

A Family Guide to

The Catholic Youth Bible

LISA-MARIE CALDERONE-STEWART

SAINT MARY'S PRESS
CHRISTIAN BROTHERS PUBLICATIONS
WINONA, MINNESOTA

Genuine recycled paper with 10% post-consumer waste.
Printed with soy-based ink.

The publishing team included Leif Kehrwald, consulting editor; Robert P. Stamschror, development editor; Brooke E. Saron, copy editor; Barbara Bartelson, production editor; Hollace Storkel, typesetter; Cindi Ramm, cover designer; produced by the graphics division of Saint Mary's Press.

Printed in the United States of America

Printing: 9 8 7 6 5 4 3 2 1

Year: 2008 07 06 05 04 03 02 01 00

ISBN 0-88489-648-X

Library of Congress Cataloging-in-Publication Data

Calderone-Stewart, Lisa-Marie.
    Know it! Pray it! Live it!: a family guide to the Catholic youth Bible / Lisa-Marie Calderone-Stewart.
        p. cm.
        ISBN 0-88489-648-X
1. Catholic youth—Religious life. 2. Christian life—Biblical teaching. [1. Catholics. 2. Christian life. 3. Conduct of life.]
I. Title: Know it!. II. Title: Pray it!. III. Title: Live it!.
IV. Title.
BX2355 .C32 2000
248.8'3—dc21
                                        00-008246
                                        CIP

This book is dedicated to
Michael James Stewart and Ralph Pierre Stewart IV

First junior high, and then senior high. For quite a while, we were the perfect "youth ministry family," equipped with our own teenagers. Me at the diocese, Dad at the parish.

Our best stuff came after field-testing it at home. Stories of your personal ups and downs found their way into books and workshops. It's about time someone gives you credit, right?

Well, this is a thank-you for being so patient with us . . . for trying out the new prayers, the new stories, and the new activities . . . for giving us your opinions on what would and would not work with a youth group . . . for having one of your parents along at practically every retreat and church event you attended . . . for standing up at the microphone at youth congresses and youth-led workshops . . . for having your words quoted by your proud parents, who were trying to be youth advocates . . . for being youth leaders . . . for being good sports . . . for being good sons. You have helped us break new ground in youth ministry. You taught us what family means. You taught us what love looks like.

Author Acknowledgments

Thank you, Mom!

> *God loves nothing so much as the person who lives with wisdom.*
> *She is more beautiful that the sun,*
> *and excels every constellation of the stars.*
>
> *(Wis 7.28–29)*

Thank you, Ralph!

> *I take pleasure in three things,*
> *and they are beautiful in the sight of God and of mortals:*
> *agreement among brothers and sisters, friendship among neighbors,*
> *and a wife and a husband who live in harmony.*
>
> *(Sir 25.1)*

Thank you, Leif Kehrwald and Bob Stamschror!

> *I thank my God every time I remember you, constantly praying with joy in every one of my prayers for all of you, because of your sharing in the gospel from the first day until now. (Phil 1.3–5)*

Thank you, Bishop Ken Untener!

> *Go in peace, daughter, and may I hear a good report about you as long as I live. (Tob 10.12)*

Contents

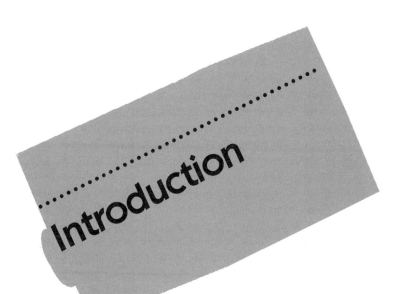

Introduction

It's time to explore *The Catholic Youth Bible (CYB)*!

This is the book for you and your family! It's for you if you are a teenager. It's for you if you are the parent of a teenager. It's for you even if you aren't a teenager or a teenager's parent! As long as you know a teenager, or like teenagers, or once were a teenager, this is a book that you will enjoy and learn from. With seven easy-to-read chapters, this book will help you explore biblical themes that relate to life's questions. How easy are these chapters? Just take a look at this!

Overview of the Seven Chapters

Each of the seven chapters asks a major life question and looks at a cluster of major biblical themes that relate to the question:

CHAPTER 1: WHY ARE WE HERE?

Themes: covenant, creation, Advent, Christmas, birth, Baptism, new life, water

CHAPTER 2: HOW DO WE LIVE?

Themes: Reign of God, teachings and advice, salt and light

CHAPTER 3: HOW LONG DOES IT TAKE?

Themes: waiting, patience, desert, Lent, suffering, time, sand

CHAPTER 4: WHY DO WE DIE?

Themes: sin and salvation, reconciliation, paschal mystery, life after death, seeds

CHAPTER 5: HOW DO WE MAKE A COMEBACK?

Themes: mission and discipleship, power of the Spirit, Confirmation, wind

CHAPTER 6: WHAT ARE WE CALLED TO BE?

Themes: social justice, human concerns, dignity of the person, globe

CHAPTER 7: WHO IS GOD?

Themes: revelation of God, images of God, the Eucharist

The Chapter Pattern

Each chapter follows the same pattern, with the same six sections:

REAL LIFE

Each chapter begins with real life situations of teenagers that relate to the chapter question and the chapter themes. For example, the letters and e-mails in chapter 1 relate to the chapter's question, Why are we here?

Sometimes the opening situations are from one point of view, and other times from several points of view. Sometimes one person talks, and other times several people talk. All the situations are straight out of real teen life.

A CLOSER LOOK

Next the chapter takes a closer look at the issues raised, and how it pertains to themes of faith that relate to the chapter's question. Catholic beliefs about these themes are explained in simple language, challenging you to dig a little deeper into what the story is really about.

IN THE BIBLE

At this point the material urges you to jump right into the Bible to examine a story or passage that deals with the chapter's questions and faith themes. It breaks open the Scriptures by connecting them to real modern day issues and exploring what God's word in the Scriptures says about them.

Check It Out

As you probably know already, the *CYB* is filled with articles, maps, charts, and indexes to help you better understand the Scriptures. This section of each chapter is filled with Scripture passages that relate to the chapter's topic or issue. You are encouraged to identify and investigate what those other related Scripture passages and articles are all about.

What Next?

Take action! This is the part of each chapter that helps you take some action based on what you have thought about, talked about, and learned thus far. Ideas for family activities are given, but naturally, you can do some of the activities by yourself or with teen or adult friends. And of course you don't have to do all the activities suggested, but having lots of ideas does make it easier to choose. Do whatever sounds good to you!

Take Time to Pray

After all that talking and reading and thinking and learning, it is time to pray. This section gives you an easy-to-do prayer that you can pray as a family. Teens or parents can also pray it alone, with a friend, or with a group.

How Does a Family Use This Book?

We hope families will use this book together, and that can happen in several ways:

You (parents and teenagers) might decide to sit down on the couch and look through one of the chapters together, as a family, discussing important ideas as you move along. Or you may decide each to go through a particular chapter alone, and then later get together to discuss what you learned. You can discuss each section, and use some of the reflection questions in the "What Next?" section to guide your discussion. Maybe you will even make some plans together based on your insights and conversations. Or perhaps you'll get involved in one of the projects listed in the "What Next?" section. The prayer in "Take Time to Pray" is good to do together but can be done separately, no matter where or when it fits in.

If you are looking for a longer plan with more details, you might consider this week-by-week outline:

Week 1: As a family you choose to do one chapter together. (You could start at the beginning of the guide with chapter 1, but you might want to start with chapter 3 if Lent is just beginning, or chapter 5 if Pentecost is around the corner.) Each of you borrows this book on a different night and separately reads the opening story, the section called "Real Life." Once you all have had a chance to read it, you gather at the dinner table and discuss the story and its character.

Week 2: Each of you borrows the book on a different night again and reads "A Closer Look." After that you all gather at the dinner table to discuss.

Week 3: Each of you borrows the book again on a different night and reads "In the Bible," looking up the passage mentioned in that section, as well as any relevant articles in the *CYB*. After you all have done the reading, you discuss it, perhaps this time in the living room. The *CYB* and this guide might be passed around and referred to throughout your discussion.

Weeks 4, 5, and 6: Over the next three weeks, you each pick a different Scripture passage from the "Check It Out" section, and read it along with any related *CYB* articles. When you gather as a family during these weeks, each of you talks about the Scripture you read and how it relates to the overall themes your family has been discussing. By reflecting and reviewing this way, you will teach one another.

Week 7: Each of you might separately read the "What's Next?" section, and then come together to express your ideas of what else you'd like to do as a family. You could do this at the dinner table, in the living room, or anywhere else. You may want to research a bit to learn what your parish and community already have going.

Week 8: You may take one evening to do the "Take Time for Prayer" section together. One of you might collect all the needed supplies and create a conducive atmosphere.

Weeks 9, 10, etc: Your family may get involved in whatever projects you chose during week 7. The length of time your project(s) take depends on what you choose, and how involved you get. Your family might decide to begin another chapter in a week or two or a month or two . . . whenever everyone seems ready to start on a different theme.

So Let's Get Started!

You don't have to start at the beginning of this book, but that is a good place to launch your studies! Actually, you can start with any chapter— maybe the one whose question strikes you the strongest. But once you decide on a chapter, you should try to walk through it until the end.

So . . . congratulations on choosing to explore *The Catholic Youth Bible!* Here's hoping that your new Bible and this new family guide will help you appreciate the word of God more fully as a family (whether you are a teenager, a teenager's parent, or otherwise!).

CHAPTER 1

Why Are We Here?

Real Life

....
LOVE LETTER SAVED IN A BABY BOOK IN OHIO

My dear precious child,

I just found out that you exist! I haven't even told your father yet! I can't wait until he comes home!

I never thought being pregnant would ever feel like this!

You are a tiny, still unnoticeable, marvelous person, living inside my body. I don't even know if you are a boy or a girl, or when I will see you for the first time. But knowing that you are alive fills me with such incredible joy! I know in my heart of hearts that I already love you deeply.

Your delighted mother

....
ENTRY FOUND IN A TEENAGER'S DIARY IN NEW HAMPSHIRE

Dear Diary,

Another boring day. Another party I didn't get invited to. Another boring weekend with nothing to do. At least I have an English paper to write. Maybe I should read one of the book assignments. Maybe I should dye my hair orange. Maybe I should get a tattoo. Maybe I should get a life.

Robin

....
ONGOING CYBERSPACE CONVERSATION FROM OREGON

Subject: Nothing much
    From: <randyk@st.francis.edu>
      To: tkoppers@aul.con

Hi, Sistwerp. What's new? Got a roommate. Todd. He's got a TV, so he's okay by me. This week I'm thinking English major. Maybe theater arts. Either that or chem premed. (Ha, ha—just joking.) Don't miss you already! And don't take any of my stuff while I'm away at college!

Randy

Subject: Nothing much
From: <tkoppers@aul.con>
To: randyk@st.francis.edu

Hi, dandy Randy. Can't wait to meet Todd. Is he a hunk, a nerd, a jock, what? Details, I need details. Something to live for now that the end of the world is coming. Wait till you hear the news—Mom is PREGNANT! I would think after two kids, she'd be happy enough. I can't believe Mom and Dad actually do it! I mean *still!* I mean do they do it when I'm actually home? This is too much to take. My life is over.

Tish

From Ohio

My dear precious child,

You started to kick! What an amazing feeling! Even your father can feel it! Can you hear us when we sing to you? Do you know how much we love you? Now that I am showing, everyone I meet asks me when you are due! See, the whole world wants to know about you!

Your delighted mother

From New Hampshire

Dear Diary,

This weekend didn't turn out to be so boring after all! I met up with Sam Cowdrey—the boy I had a crush on in first grade! He moved away. I thought he moved out of the country, but he only moved out of the school district! He was at the mall! How come I never saw him all these years? He's just the same, but older and cuter. We're going to a movie tomorrow night! I wonder if his friends will like my friends. Who cares?

Robin

....
FROM OREGON

Subject: The family news
    From: <randyk@st.francis.edu>
        To: tkoppers@aul.con

Sistwerp, relax. What's the big deal? So Mom and Dad still do it. So what? Let them have some fun. They don't get out much, you know. Wonder what Mom will look like fat. Do we get to put in our vote for a name? How about Zenith or Moon or Polaris. Maybe I'll major in astronomy.

Randy

Subject: The family news
    From: <tkoppers@aul.con>
        To: randyk@st.francis.edu

Randy Blandy. What do you mean, "What's the big deal?" Not only will Mom get fat (and everyone will say dumb things like, "Tish, is your mom pregnant or just fat or what?") but she'll get tired and cranky, and I'll have to do all the house-cleaning, and then once the baby comes, I'll have to do all the baby-sitting. My social life is over! They better not make me change stinky diapers! Don't you see the big picture? It doesn't affect you at all! (Except for one thing: Guess whose room gets turned into a kiddy nursery! Not mine 'cause I'm still here!)

Tish

....
FROM OHIO

My precious child,
    I wish I had words to explain my feelings. It won't be long now. . . . We are past the halfway mark! If you are a girl, you will be named Hope Claire. If you are a boy, you will be named Kenneth Joseph.
    We have your room ready. Daddy painted it and everyone is filling it with teddy bears. You even have a closet of clothes and blankets waiting for you.
    Your cousins and grandparents and aunts and uncles pray for you every day. So do we. I love you so much.

Your delighted mommy

From New Hampshire

Dear Diary,

I love Sam! I knew it in first grade! I didn't tell him yet about my missed period. I'm going to wait awhile to be sure. I didn't tell anyone. I just love Sam so much, I don't want this to ruin it. I'm so scared. What if it's true? I don't know what to do.

Robin

From Oregon

Subject: Sara
From: <tkoppers@aul.con>
To: randyk@st.francis.edu

Randy, Randy, Randy! She is gorgeous! When are you coming home? I can't believe you've waited this long! Mom got out our baby pictures—Sara looks just like me! Mom still has all my baby dresses, and now Sara can wear them! Mom is a little tired still, but she's doing all right. She lets me hold Sara and give her a bottle and burp her and let her sleep on my lap. She is a doll! Tiny, itty-bitty fingernails and toes! The softest skin! I guess I never saw a baby up close before! Dad already took three rolls of pictures. When are you coming home? You'll have to sleep on the couch, of course, but I hope that's not stopping you. Mom and Dad would like to see you. Don't you want to see Sara before she grows up? Gotta go. I hear her fussing.

Tish

Subject: Sara
From: <randyk@st.francis.edu>
To: tkoppers@aul.con

Hi, Sistwerps.

Sara: Don't let Tish drop you or do something stupid like that. Tish: Since I'm the guest when I come home, I believe you'll be on the couch, and I'll get a bed! Tell Mom and Dad I'll be there this weekend. I guess I'm a proud big brother! Gotta go. I hear Todd fussing.

Randy

....
From Ohio

Dear Ken and Hope,

You two are beautiful! I must admit, when the doctor told me you would be twins, we were surprised. But we don't have to worry much! You have so many people in your lives already! With all this help, it's like being on vacation!

Daddy and I are just overjoyed. We can't stop smiling! You will be baptized on the feast of the guardian angels! And I know now there were two angels watching over this pregnancy, just as I have two angels of my own to hold and cuddle.

God bless my two precious angels.

Your delighted mommy

....
From New Hampshire

Dear Diary,

I hate Sam. I will never speak to him again. I will never see him again. I can't believe what he said. He never loved me. He didn't want to hear about how I felt. He didn't want to know what I thought. He just wanted me to "get rid of my problem." I feel so sick I could just die. Maybe I should die.

I can't believe they just did it to me. I didn't know it would hurt. I thought it was going to be easier.

I didn't know I would feel so guilty. I'm taking some pills tonight. If I'm not here tomorrow, this will be the last time I write. I hate myself.

Robin

A Closer Look

Why are we here, anyway? Why is anybody here? Why is anything here? Why is there *something* rather than *nothing*? Why is there anybody rather than nobody? God is why. God is the answer. "God is love" (1 Jn 4.16).

You can't love someone if there are no someones to love, so God decided to create us in order to love us. And so that we might love God and one another. Of course, love can't be forced. Love, by definition, is free. I can't make you love me. But I can love you even if you never love me.

So people are created in a way that makes them capable of loving and capable of creating more people. That's the main idea, anyway. And that is the main idea of the Creation stories in Genesis, the first book of the Bible. The Creation stories are the result of a lot of reflection on God and life, a lot of struggle to figure it all out, and a lot of faith.

Notice that the first sentence of the Bible mentions water. In the very beginning, before there were people, before there were animals, before there was light, there was water (see Gen 1.1–2). In our own personal beginning, before we were born, before we saw people or animals or even light, there was also water. Perhaps you have heard the story of how you or someone else was born. Perhaps you have heard about where a mother was when her water broke.

Before we were born, we were surrounded by water in our mother's womb. We would float and rock and sway with her movement. That is one reason why infants love to be held and rocked.

As a mother cradles her child, sings lullabies, and feeds her baby, she is expressing her covenant of love. She is saying, I am your mother, and you are my child. You came from me, and I love you. I will take care of you. I will not leave you. You can trust me. You are safe with me.

In a similar way, God makes a covenant with us. God is our parent, and we are God's people. We are children of God (see 1 Jn 2.29—3.3). Our relationship with God continues to grow, just as our relationship with our own mother or father continues to grow as we mature.

In the Bible

In chapter 6 of Genesis, God is displeased with the wickedness of humankind, but God is pleased with Noah. So God decides to wash out all the evil of the world with a tremendous flood. God tells Noah to build an ark, a large boat, and to load up his extended family, plenty of food, and a pair of every species of animal. The flood destroys everything and everyone except for those in the ark.

Eventually the rain stops, the sun comes out, and the waters subside. God calls the people out of the ark, and Noah builds an altar and offers a sweet-smelling sacrifice to God. God sends a rainbow as a symbol of God's covenant with Noah and all his descendants. Never again will God set out to destroy life. God says, "Be fruitful and multiply, and fill the earth" (Gen 1.28), the very same words God speaks in the first Creation story. With water comes the birth of a new way of life, a life of people in covenant with God.

People are told that they can trust God; they can rest safely in God's arms. As a mother cradles her infant, as the waters of the flood lifted up the ark, God will hold us and love us. That is the covenant of love that God has made with us.

Check It Out

The story of the Great Flood begins in chapter 6 of Genesis and continues through chapter 9. You can read the whole story, along with related articles, in the *CYB*.

The Bible is filled with passages about pregnancy, about the mystery of birth, about the depth of a mother's love, and about God's covenant with us. The following lists present some other Scripture passages and articles from the *CYB* that you might check out as you explore those themes more deeply:

PREGNANCY STORIES

- Hagar conceives. (Gen 16.1–14)
- Sarah's pregnancy is foretold. (Gen 18.1–15)
- Rebekah's twins struggle in the womb. (Gen 25.21–28)
- Samson's birth is foretold. (Judges, chapter 13; 1 Sam 1.1—2.11)
- John's birth is foretold. (Lk 1.5–25)
- Jesus' birth is foretold. (Lk 1.26–38)
- Mary visits Elizabeth. (Lk 1.39–56)

BIRTH STORIES

- Sarah gives birth. (Gen 21.1–7)
- Moses is born and hidden. (Ex 1.8—2.10)
- John is born to Elizabeth. (Lk 1.57–80)
- Jesus is born to Mary. (Mt 1.18–25, Lk 2.1–21)

Stories of Women Loving Their Children, of God Loving Us

- Herod kills the infants. (Mt 2.16–18)
- Rachel weeps for her children. (Jer 31.15–17)
- "You kept me safe on my mother's breast." (Ps 22.9–11)
- "You knit me together in my mother's womb." (Ps 139.13)
- "I will not forget you." (Isa 49.15–16)

General Creation Stories

- The world is created. (Genesis, chapters 1–2)
- In the beginning was the Word. (Jon 1.1–9)
- The Old Testament view of menstruation is given. (Lev 15.19–32)
- The Old Testament view of childbirth is given. (Leviticus, chapter)

Stories of God's Covenant with Us

- God promises Abraham land and offspring. (Gen 12.1–9; Genesis, chapter 15; Gen 17.1–14)
- God gives the Ten Commandments to Moses. (Ex 19.1—20.17)
- God promises David a kingdom. (2 Sam 7.1–7)
- "I desire steadfast love and not sacrifice." (Hos 6.4–7)
- "Let justice roll down like waters, and righteousness like an ever-flowing stream." (Am 5.21–24)
- "I will be their God, they shall be my people." (Jer 31.31–34)
- God's New Covenant is realized in Jesus. (Lk 22.14–20)
- God's Covenant is extended to all people. (Romans, chapters 9–10)
- Christ is a sacrifice, a high priest, and the New Covenant. (Hebrews, chapters 8–10)

What Next?

What can a teenager do with his or her family to further explore the themes of covenant, creation, Advent, Christmas, birth, Baptism, new life, and water? Here are some starter ideas for you:

- Discuss the Scriptures. For example, look up Mt 2.16–18 and Jer 31.15–17, and the related articles in the *CYB*, all of which are about Rachel weeping. Notice how the New Testament passage has deeper meaning when you read the Old Testament passage along with it. Discuss this deeper meaning: Can you imagine the grief of a mother whose child has been killed? Do you remember the first time you learned about the Holocaust of World War II? Why does a person choose to kill another human being? How does a person who enjoys violent movies contribute to a culture's general tolerance of violence?

- Discuss the story at the beginning of this chapter. Regarding "From Oregon," what changed Tish's mind about having a baby in the house? Regarding "From Ohio," how can a loving family create a blanket of support that cradles a new mother and twins? Regarding "From New Hampshire," what are some possible consequences of irresponsible sexual activity?

- Take a look at a difficult issue: Life is precious. We all are loved by God the moment we are conceived, and God confirms that love by providing pleasure to parents while they create new life. But sometimes things don't happen perfectly. Sometimes life is conceived without love. Sometimes a woman is raped. Sometimes a pregnancy is unplanned. Sometimes an unmarried couple gets carried away, and suddenly a baby is on the way. An abortion can seem like the easiest way out of this inconvenient or embarrassing situation, but life is precious. A newly conceived life can be saved in ways that restore and include love. Discuss what you would do if you unexpectedly became the parent of an unborn child. How would you cope? Whom could you tell? What or who would be your support system? Who could help you decide what to do?

- Be a friend. Discuss how to be a friend to someone with an unwanted pregnancy, whether that someone is the father or the mother. How would you develop good listening skills? How would you be nonjudgmental? How would you avoid gossip? Figure out ahead of time what you would need to know in such a situation, and take the time now to learn it. Be prepared to help someone by knowing where to find a caring adult or professional to help if a crisis occurs. Remember to assure your friend of your loyalty. Much of the terror of an unwanted pregnancy is the fear of going it alone. Knowing someone cares can give a person the strength to get through a difficult ordeal.

- Let the symbols speak. To appreciate the wonder of pregnancy and birth, let the ordinary symbols around you speak. Pay attention when you swim, take a shower, or drink a glass of pure, cold water. Watch the waves at the beach. Think about water and birth. Talk to pregnant relatives and friends. Baby-sit for new parents. Ask questions about a birth or adoption. Listen and learn. This is a wonderful time to let the symbols speak.
- Note the reason for the season. For example, during Advent and Christmastime, we hear stories of pregnancy and birth, we celebrate Jesus having been conceived in Mary's womb and coming to us through birth as a tiny human being. What does this reveal about pregnancy and birth? What does this say in answer to the question, Why are we here?

Take Time to Pray

This prayer works well with teenagers and parents. Naturally, you also can pray it alone or with friends.

THE CALL TO PRAYER

Pour warm water into a clear bowl. Take a silent moment to get in touch with our heavenly Creator.

GOD'S WORD

Read Ps 139.1–18.

REFLECTION

Life is precious. You are loved in the womb long before you have a name or a face. You are wonderfully made, and God sings with joy for you. You do not come into this world alone. You are born through a woman, arriving with water and blood. You are greeted at the end of your birth canal with eager, waiting hands. You are immediately held and cuddled and rocked and wrapped. You still cry because everything is so new and overwhelming. And you grow and learn and change. And God never stops loving you. We are a covenant people, bound together by love.

BLESSING

Swirl your fingers around in the bowl of water. Ask the almighty Creator of the oceans, lakes, and rivers to bless the water. Bless yourself. Sprinkle one another with the water, or make a small cross on one another's foreheads to signify your covenant with God and with one another.

CHAPTER 2

How Do We Live?

Real Life

MR. MARTINEZ (TO HIMSELF):

Aaron is that new sophomore. He's not very noticeable, but I've observed that he's alone a lot, trying not to be noticed. He hasn't exactly found a bunch of friends to hang out with, so he spends every lunch hour trying to be invisible. But he's good in class. Either he studies hard, or he has a natural gift for talking off-the-cuff. Amazing that he can be so confident in class and so awkward walking around, trying to blend with the wallpaper.

AARON (TO HIMSELF):

I'm not so sure I like this new school. I know I'm supposed to give it time, but how much time? It's boring to walk around all day and pretend to have friends. No one takes the initiative. No one says hello. No one cares. I wish I were a basketball star so I could just walk onto the team and dazzle everyone. I wish I were really rich so I could drive up in my sporty car and impress everyone. I wish I had some talent that people would notice. I wish there were some people who wanted to be my friends.

MR. MARTINEZ AND AARON:

"Aaron, can I talk with you a minute?"
"Sure, Mr. Martinez. What's up?"
"Aaron, I'd like you to join a group we're forming here at school."
"What kind of group?"
"It's a group that will be trained in conflict resolution."
"What's that?"
"Conflict resolution is a way of settling disagreements peacefully. You know, without violence, without fighting. Just by talking things out. We will train you to present a workshop to kids at some of the area middle schools, and you can get class credit for presenting the workshops. Maybe we'll do one presentation a month. How does that sound?"
"Okay, sure."

"Here's some information for your parents to look over and sign. It explains the whole program, the dates, everything. Bring it back tomorrow and we'll be all set."

"Thanks for asking me, Mr. Martinez."

"Aaron, I just think you'll do very well in this workshop group. Thanks for saying yes."

....
MR. MARTINEZ (TO HIMSELF):

Well, that training went really well! I was amazed at these kids. They picked up on everything so easily. That Aaron is a natural leader! Two seniors, eight juniors, and six sophomores. Not exactly a balanced group, but it sure seemed to work. Starting this leadership group was a great idea.

....
AARON (TO HIMSELF):

Wow, that was fun! At first I didn't think it would be so much fun. I was sorry I said yes right away. What was I thinking? I was worried! What was I getting into? But those kids were really great! I think I have fifteen new friends! This is the best thing I've done since we moved to this town!

....
MR. MARTINEZ AND AARON:

"Aaron, what's going on here? Where's the fight?"

"There's no fight, Mr. Martinez. Everything's okay here."

"Then why did three screaming girls come running into my office to tell me about the fight?"

"Well, maybe there was *almost* a fight, but everything's figured out now."

"What was the problem?"

"I wasn't here when it started, but I think Chet and Pedro had a misunderstanding. Something about somebody's watch, and then their cars, their girlfriends, then some nasty insults, and everyone was ready to start fighting."

"Where is everyone?"

"Chet and Pedro calmed down, and Gary showed up with the watch, and I guess they just worked it out. You can go talk to them. They're in the parking lot now. But I don't think they're angry anymore. Well, maybe a little, but not enough to fight."

"Thanks, Aaron, I will go talk to them."

MR. MARTINEZ (TO HIMSELF):

Wow. Pedro and Chet? A fight that didn't happen? Those two have hated each other for three years. Ever since Pedro stole Chet's girlfriend. Or did Chet steal Pedro's girlfriend? Well, not that anyone can actually *steal* anyone's girlfriend.

But now I understand why those girls were so hysterical. I'd just better be sure everything is over. Aaron did a heck of a job! That peacemaking stuff really works! I'm impressed big time! Wait till I tell the principal about this!

AARON (TO HIMSELF):

Wow. That conflict resolution stuff really works! I was sure mad when Chet insulted Gloria like that. And I don't know Stacey, but Pedro said some nasty things about her. No wonder they were ready to kill each other. I wanted to punch both of them on the spot. But I can't do that anymore—they all know I'm on the peacemaking team. I couldn't insult them back, I couldn't threaten them, I couldn't do any of those things, or I'd lose my credibility with the team. I had to try those new skills and hope that they would work. I mean, wow! It happened just like we practiced! That peacemaking stuff is awesome!

A Closer Look

How are we supposed to live? Should every day be a struggle? Is our job to compete with the rest of the world and win the daily contest? Do we have to prove that we are the best, the smartest, the greatest looking, or the most trendy? Is that how it works?

Jesus says no. Jesus says the last will be first (see Lk 13.30). The losers will be winners. The ones who don't enter the contest are the ones who will be victorious. The ones not climbing the ladder of success will be the most successful. In the Reign of God, sometimes called the Kingdom of Heaven or the Kingdom of God, it's the little things that make a big heart.

But take a look at our world. Turn on the television or the radio. In between songs and sitcoms about failing relationships, nowhere jobs, and family stress, you hear commercials—commercials for products that reinforce how your hair isn't full enough, how your stomach isn't firm enough, how your clothes aren't trendy enough, and how this toothpaste, deodorant, shampoo, you-name-it is just what you need to turn your life around.

We are constantly told that we must compete for an artificial ideal that is almost impossible to attain. Even models have their pictures airbrushed or computer enhanced for advertisements and commercials. If someone who is hired for his or her looks isn't perfect enough to showcase, how is it possible for the rest of us to get the look we are all supposed to be striving for?

It's a scam. It's a setup. It's a trap to get money from consumers. And we're so gullible that we're buying it! We put so much time, effort, and money into trying to put together the right look, that by the time we almost have it, it has changed! Advertisers do that on purpose! They keep changing the right look so that we will keep buying things, so that we can't ever truly achieve the goal.

We have become a greedy, materialistic society. Gimmee, gimmee. I gotta have it. Jesus tells us there is another way—a better way. In fact, his followers were originally called followers of the Way, long before they were called Christians.

This is good news. We don't have to compete. We don't have to fight. We don't have to run the race to outbuy one another. We can be humble. We can be childlike. We can be happy with who we are. It's less stressful. It's more fulfilling. It's more peaceful. And it makes more sense.

In the Bible

In Matthew's Gospel, the Sermon on the Mount (see Matthew, chapters 5–7) begins when Jesus climbs up a mountainside and teaches. Some of Jesus' most famous words are recorded here.

The first part of the Gospel is called the Beatitudes. Webster's dictionary defines *beatitude* as "a state of utmost bliss" and *beatify* as "to make supremely happy." In the Beatitudes Jesus describes the people who are the most happy, the most blessed, and in fact, the luckiest.

So who are these people who are so lucky, so blessed, and so happy? They are not rich, aggressive, proud, successful, victorious, ambitious, or fashionable people! They are poor in spirit and depressed. They are those who cry their eyes out. They are those who mourn, those who are sad, those who are heartbroken. They are meek and humble. They are those who are stepped on in life. They are those who hunger and thirst for righteousness, those who want goodness. They are merciful. They are those who forgive, those who are compassionate. They are pure in heart. They are those who are honest, those who don't manipulate or control. They are the peacemakers, those who try to work things out, not fight things out. They are those who are persecuted, those who are mocked and called names. These are the lucky ones! The happy ones! The blessed ones! Why on earth would Jesus say this? How could this be true? Because these people shall see God, because they are children of God, because they will inherit the earth, because theirs is the Kingdom of God, the Reign of God. The Beatitudes are the way of Jesus.

Check It Out

The Sermon on the Mount is recorded in Matthew, chapters 5–7; you can read the whole sermon, along with related articles, in the *CYB*.

The Bible is filled with passages that describe the Reign of God, give helpful advice for peaceful and happy living, and provide good general teachings. The following lists present some other Scripture passages and articles from the *CYB* that you might check out as you explore those themes more deeply:

PROVERBS AND SAYINGS FROM THE SAGES OF THE OLD TESTAMENT

- true security for tough times (Prov 3.21–26)
- laziness (Prov 6.6–11)
- gossip (Prov 11.13)
- integrity (Prov 28.6)

- God of all seasons (Eccl 3.8)
- honoring parents (Sir 3.1–7)
- friends (Sir 6.5–17)
- ruining reputations (Sir 28.12–18)
- irresponsible drinking (Sir 31.25–31)

LAWS AND COMMANDMENTS

- the Ten Commandments (Ex 20.1–17, Deut 5.1–21)
- the greatest commandment (Deut 6.4–9, Mt 22.36–38)

TEACHINGS OF JESUS

- salt of the earth, light of the world (Mt 5.13–16)
- the Lord's Prayer (Mt 6.5–15, Lk 11.1–4)
- welcoming children (Mt 19.13–15, Mk 10.13–16, Lk 18.15–17)
- "Woe to you." (Mt 23.13–36)
- "Who is the greatest?" (Mt 18.1–5, Mk 9.33–37, Lk 9.46–48)
- blessings and woes (Lk 6.20–26)
- "I am the bread of life." (Jn 6.35–40)
- gate for sheep, good shepherd (Jn 10.1–18)
- "I am the way, and the truth, and the life." (Jn 14.6–7)
- vine and branches (Jn 15.1–11)
- "Love one another." (Jn 15.12–17)

PARABLES ABOUT THE REIGN OF GOD

- Check out the events, people, and teaching index on page 1510 of the *CYB*—the parables are all listed alphabetically there.

PASSAGES ABOUT THE REIGN OF GOD

- the Garden of Eden (Gen 2.4–3.24)
- Jerusalem and Zion, symbols of God's Kingdom (Psalm 132)
- Isaiah prophesies a messianic kingdom. (Isa 11.1–9)
- a messianic kingdom (Isa 61.1–2, Lk 4.16–21)
- Saint Paul describes God's Reign. (1 Cor 15.24–27)
- a promise of a new creation, God's Reign (Rev 21.1—22.5)

What Next?

What can a teenager do with her or his family to further explore the Reign of God, the teachings of Jesus, the helpful advice of the Old and New Testaments, and salt and light? Here are some starter ideas for you:

- Discuss the Scriptures. For example, look up Mt 6.5–15 and Lk 11.1–4, and the related articles in the *CYB*, all of which are about the Lord's Prayer. The article in Matthew has good reflection questions for you to talk about. Also discuss the personal history behind this prayer: Where did you first hear of this prayer? How did you learn it? Who taught it to you? Now that you are older, how has your understanding of the prayer changed?

- Discuss the story at the beginning of this chapter. What kinds of things do you think Aaron learned in his conflict resolution workshop that would be helpful in mediating two angry enemies ready to fight? What are some basic communication skills that might help people work it out rather than fight it out?

- Take a look at a difficult issue: Violence is everywhere. Even children have begun to pick up on the television shows, movies, and video games that depict violent lifestyles as normal. Shoot-outs are happening at schools, and children are not only the victims but also the perpetrators. Often, where violence is out of control, so are the use and abuse of alcohol and other drugs. When people are drunk or high, violence may not seem far-fetched. Discuss the situation in your school and neighborhood regarding the use of alcohol and other drugs and violence and other crimes. Are your school and neighborhood safe places? How many friends do you have that get drunk or high sometimes or often? Have you tried drinking or using other drugs? Do you do so regularly? Does anyone you know drink and drive, or use other drugs and then drive? Have you ever ridden with a drunk or high driver? Have you driven while drunk or high? These are serious issues to address. Injury, death, and jail time are possible consequences when unhealthy situations get out of hand and violence takes place.

- Be a friend. Develop good, healthy habits. Stay away from alcohol and other drugs, and stay away from guns and other weapons. Tell your friends about your decision to remain healthy and safe, and support them as they try to do the same. If someone brings alcohol or other drugs to a party, refuse to stay. If you don't have access to a car, or if the person who drove you has been drinking or using drugs, then call your parents or a reliable friend.

If you have friends that are already experimenting with alcohol and other drugs, talk to some responsible, professional adults about what your options are. You might be able to influence your friends, but sometimes it's safer not to try. Sometimes it's best just to find other friends in order to avoid risky situations altogether.

- Let the symbols speak. Pay careful attention to advice in newspapers and magazines. Notice what television commercials and magazine ads are trying to sell you. Look at what you have in your own house. Are you being brainwashed by the media? Or are you following the way of Jesus?
- Note the reason for the season. In the Mass readings during ordinary time, we hear a lot about Jesus' teachings. In this case, *ordinary* doesn't mean "plain and boring," *ordinary* means "ordered" or "counted," as in Fifth Sunday of Ordinary Time, Thirty-fifth Sunday of Ordinary Time, and so on. Listen to the advice that Jesus gives in the Sunday Scripture readings during this time.

Take Time to Pray

This prayer works well with teenagers and parents together. Naturally you can pray it alone or with friends.

THE CALL TO PRAYER

Light a candle and pour a small amount of salt into a dish. Take a moment to get in touch with Jesus, our savior.

GOD'S WORD

Read Mt 5.13–16.

REFLECTION

You are light. You are so bright, Jesus asks you to shine your light for others to see. You don't need special tooth whiteners for your smile to be beautiful. You don't need special hair sparklers for your soul to shine. You don't need fancy new clothes to show off your personality. Jesus already wants your light to shine.

You are salt. You are not bland. You are not invisible. You are so salty that Jesus asks you to share your life so that others can have flavor. You don't need trendy new shoes for your feet to take you places. You don't need designer labels to get into the Kingdom of Heaven. You don't need expensive perfumes or colognes to enhance your style. Jesus already wants your flavor for life to be shared.

Nothing you see on television commercials can improve your salt factor. Nothing you read in magazine ads can increase your light factor. You cannot buy inner peace. You cannot buy your way into the Reign of God. Jesus asks you to live a simple life and to follow his way. Jesus wants you to live as the salt of the earth and the light for the world.

BLESSING

Everyone lick one of your fingers and taste a few granules of salt. Hold up the candle. Ask Jesus to bless the salt and the candle. Pray the following prayer or a similar prayer:

Jesus, I promise that every time I see a candle or taste salt, I will try to remember to be light for the world and salt for the earth. Amen.

CHAPTER 3

How Long Does It Take?

Real Life

Story 1

The young man fingered the pages of his achievement portfolio. He liked the way each page felt, printed on card stock, inside a plastic sleeve. He liked the way the pages looked as well, printed by his new color printer, a purchase he made after high school with the money he saved from years of working at the car wash.

His mother came downstairs. "What are you doing? Still admiring your portfolio? Did you think your binder was going to look that impressive when you first started to put it together?" She rubbed her hand along his back, waiting for a response.

"No. Yes. I don't know. Sometimes it seems that I have done so much more in high school than my brother or sister did. Other times I look at all these pages and I think, So what? Is this really going to get me into college? Is this really going to get me the scholarships I need?"

She tried to comfort him. "Well, honey, you did a good job showcasing all of your talents and abilities. You sent in all your applications, requested all the transcripts, and got all the necessary recommendations. You should feel proud of all your accomplishments! Dad and I are mighty proud of you! The time will pass. You can't speed it up. Sooner or later, the mail will bring you the news you are waiting for. There's nothing else you can do now but wait it out and try not to think about it too much."

Her words weren't much comfort. Not thinking about it would be difficult. This was the rest of his life! How could he not think about it? But she was right. All he could do now was wait it out.

Story 2

The young woman fingered the fabric of his denim jacket. It smelled like him. She loved his scent, and she closed her eyes and buried her face into its folds, breathing in all that was him.

Then she opened her eyes and was slapped with reality. She was in a hospital room, watching her best friend, her soul mate, fight for his life. He was unconscious, hooked up to machines that quietly purred and beeped, monitored and fed, breathed and supported.

At the time, she was alone with him, but soon someone else would appear. His family and closest friends had organized a vigil of watching and taking a break, so that he would never be alone. That way everyone wanting to be there with him would also get a chance to go home for a little while and try to rest and make an effort to sleep.

His brother came into the room. "How are you doing?" (That's what everyone kept asking one another.) "I'm fine." (That's what everyone kept answering.) It didn't say much, but it cut the silence nicely.

"The driver died. The nurse just told me. We'll never be able to ask him why he got into a car, knowing how drunk he was. We'll never be able to tell him what he did to our family. I wonder if he knows about the nightmare he's caused. I wonder if he even knew that he hit someone."

She shrugged. "Somehow, I think he knows. If he is dead now, he knows."

He put his arm around her, and she felt tears well up in her eyes again. She thought by now all the tears would have been drained out. She was surprised that she had any left.

He tried to comfort her. "Hey, why don't you try to get some rest? My dad is on his way up. He can give you a ride home, or to our house, if you want. Mom just got home. I know she's still up. When I left, she was looking through his scrapbooks and baby books and all that stuff. I don't know why she's doing that now. It seems like torture to me. Why rub it in? Why make the suffering any worse than it already is? The doctors are doing everything they can do. The time will pass. We can't speed it up. There's nothing we can do now, but wait it out and try not to worry too much."

His words weren't much comfort. Not worrying would be impossible! This was her soul mate's life they were talking about! This was her life they were talking about, too! How could she not worry? But he was right. All she could do now was wait it out.

Story 3

The young woman fingered the fabric of her shirt. Inmate orange. She always hated orange. Now she wears it every day—a symbol of how she hates her life. How did she get here? It's still unreal. She never thought she was capable of murder. She still doesn't think she committed murder.

But that's why she is in jail. After all, her husband is dead, and she's the one who killed him. Does that make it murder?

No, she reasons. She didn't commit murder. She was not trying to end a life. She was trying to save a life. She and her daughter had been abused continually since her daughter was born. Sooner or later he would have killed one of them. Or both of them. It could have happened that very night. She had to stop him. She couldn't let him hurt them again.

Everything moved so quickly. She hardly knew what she was doing. He came after them in the kitchen. She grabbed the knife, and all she remembered next was blood everywhere, her daughter screaming and crying. She called 911. Do murderers do that?

Now they're going to try to take her baby away. She's got to stop them. They have to believe her story. They have to understand that this man is a monster. He looks like a saint, but he is a monster. He even fooled her, or she would never have married him.

"Hi."

The word startles her. It is the chaplain. The only visitor she wants to see. How can she look into anyone else's eyes after what she has done? The chaplain didn't know her before, so he feels no pain, no disappointment when he looks at her.

"I just spoke with your lawyer. She thinks you have a good case."

Good case. Whatever that means.

"She said your daughter has been asking about you day and night. They are going to try to arrange a visit."

Try to arrange a visit. My little girl needs me. Why can't they just bring her here? I'm not going to hurt her! I was trying to protect her! How hard is it to arrange a visit?

He tries to comfort her.

"Listen. You were very articulate, explaining your situation to me and to the lawyer. You are in very capable hands. She knows what she is doing. I agree with her. You have a good case. I don't think you will be here much longer. She'll call you as soon as there's news to tell. The time will pass. You can't speed it up. There's nothing else you can do now but wait it out and try not to dwell on it too much."

His words aren't much comfort. "Try not to dwell on it" is ridiculous advice! This is the rest of her life! This is the rest of her baby's life! How can she not dwell on it? But the chaplain is right. All she can do now was wait it out.

A Closer Look

How long can we stand all this waiting?

Hurry up and wait! God's time is not our time. I demand patience, and I want it right now! God writes straight with crooked lines. Some things just take time. Rome wasn't built in a day.

Have you ever heard these sayings? They may not be much comfort, but they all come from the experience of having to wait.

Why is waiting so painful and frustrating? When we have to wait, we feel powerless, out of control, even a bit irresponsible—as if we shouldn't be standing around doing nothing. Shouldn't we be doing something? Don't just stand there! Do something!

Yet during the most powerless, frustrating times of waiting out something with someone we care about, we almost need to tell ourselves the opposite: Don't just do something! Stand there!

This is what the ministry of presence is all about. Sometimes we just can't do anything. And being willing to do nothing, being willing to stand there with another person and share that time is the best thing we can do. By simply standing there and doing nothing with someone, we convey an important message: I'm here for you. Nothing else is going to take my attention away from you. I am willing to feel some pain, endure frustration, and tolerate the anxiety that comes with this awful situation because I care about you. I can't really *do* anything to help, but I am giving you the gift of my time.

And, as you know, time takes time.

Have you ever played with a sandglass? Have you ever watched the sand granules slip down through the opening into the bottom chamber? Perhaps there's a three-minute egg timer in your kitchen or an hourglass in your living room. Nothing you do—even if you shake it—can speed up the process.

Having to stand around and do nothing while waiting for some pain to pass or some difficult situation to be over is not new to our generation! "How long, O Lord?" has been a prayer on the lips of the people of God for as long as there have been people of God. Habakkuk (1.2), Zechariah (1.12), and Isaiah (6.11) are prophets noted for this famous phrase. There's quite a bit of history tied up in this business of waiting.

The good news is that God is also willing to stand with us and wait. God's wisdom tells us that waiting time is not necessarily wasted time.

During the pain and frustration of waiting, we often do a little reflecting, frequently a little talking, and sometimes even a little praying. These things aren't bad.

This may not be much comfort, but the next time you have to hurry up and wait, or the next time you feel like demanding immediate patience, just try to remember that some things just take time, and God's time is not our time. Because after all, Rome wasn't built in a day, and sooner or later, you'll come to realize that God writes straight with crooked lines.

In the Bible

The entire book of Exodus is a story of waiting. You might say the Israelites wrote the book on waiting! It could even be called the greatest "hurry up and wait" saga in history!

At the beginning of the book, the Israelites have multiplied and grown, making the Egyptians nervous. The Egyptians oppress and punish them, but the Israelites have tremendous endurance. "How long, O Lord, must we be slaves?" is their daily prayer.

Meanwhile, Moses is born, hidden, and found; he grows up and becomes a murderer; he flees and marries; he is called back by God; he returns and becomes the hero to lead the Israelite slaves to freedom.

After ten plagues and a holy Passover supper, the Israelites escape slavery by a miraculous crossing of the Reed (or Red) Sea. They are free, but they are in the middle of the desert. "Hurry up and wait" describes their adventure perfectly. And then, "How long, O Lord, must we wander in the desert?" becomes their prayer.

The Israelites spent a lot of time in that desert. Those who were slaves as teenagers had children and then grandchildren who never knew life any other way. That's a lot of time for reflecting, for talking, and for praying.

Of all the people in the Old Testament, Moses stands out as the most significant hero by far: "He led them out, having performed wonders and signs in Egypt, at the Red Sea, and in the wilderness for forty years" (Acts 7.36). The Ten Commandments he received from God are still the moral code followed by most people in the world—Jews, Christians, and Muslims alike.

Check It Out

The book of Exodus tells the story of Moses and the long waiting the Israelites experienced. You can stroll through the book in the *CYB* and take a look at the story and the articles that go with it.

The Bible as a whole is filled with passages about waiting, patience, desert, lent, suffering, time, and sand. Here are some other Scripture passages you might check out as you explore the theme of waiting more deeply:

How Long, O Lord?

- David (Psalm 13)
- Habakkuk's vision (Heb 1.1–5)

Sabbath

- the Sabbath (Gen 2.3)
- Jubilee year (Leviticus, chapter 25)

In Prison

- Joseph (Gen 39.20—41.36)
- Jeremiah (Jeremiah, chapter 37)
- Shadrach, Meshach, and Abednego (Dan 2.46—3.97)
- John the Baptist (Mt 11.2–6; 14.1–2; Mk 6.14–29; Lk 7.18–23; 9.1–6)
- several of the Apostles (Acts 5.17–32)
- Peter (Acts 12.3–19)
- Paul and Silas (Acts of the Apostles, chapter 16)

Desert Time and Other Time Spent Waiting

- Elijah flees. (1 Kings 19.1–14)
- Ezekiel in the valley of the dry bones (Ezek 37.1–14)
- Jonah's experience (Jon 1.17—2.10)
- Jesus in the desert for forty days and nights (Mt 4.1–11, Mk 1.1–12, Lk 4.1–13)

- Jesus in the garden before his arrest (Mt 26.36–46, Mk 14.32–42, Lk 22.39–46, Jn 18.1)
- Mary Magdalene and Mary the mother of James and Joseph after Jesus' burial (Mt 27.59–61)

In Exile

- lament over the destruction of Jerusalem (Psalm 137)
- Babylonian Exile (2 Kings 17.7; 25.1)

What Next?

What can teenagers and parents do together to further explore the themes of waiting, patience, desert, lent, suffering, time, and sand. Here are some starter ideas for you:

- Discuss the Scriptures. For example, read the introduction to Exodus, Ex 14.1–31, and the articles "Look to the Hills" and "God Liberates Us from Oppression," on pages 75 and 76 of the *CYB*. Do you remember learning about the Civil War? Can you imagine what it was like to be a slave, wanting and waiting to be freed? Can you imagine having your family or friends taken away from you? Can you imagine being bought or sold, poked or prodded, inspected as an animal would be? Can you imagine having an unrealistic amount of physical labor demanded of you and no way to quit, protest, or escape? How do you think that experience would affect a person? How would it affect a whole community or population, including successive generations?
- Discuss the stories at the beginning of this chapter. What might it be like waiting to find out if you were accepted into the college of your choice? Have you, or has anyone you know, gone through this experience? What might it be like waiting to see if someone you love will recover from a coma? Have you, or has anyone you know, gone through such an experience? What might it be like waiting to see if you will spend the rest of your life in prison? What might it be like waiting to see if your children will be allowed to visit you? What might it be like waiting to hear if the jury's verdict will call for the death penalty? Have you, or has anyone you know, gone through such an experience? How

are the characters and their feelings in these three stories similar to one another? How are they different? How are they similar to or different from you and your feelings?

- Take a look at some difficult issues: Prisons and hospitals as well as nursing homes and hospice homes are institutions where pain and waiting are commonplace. Old age, physical changes resulting from injuries, particular sicknesses, and criminal records each add their own type of pain to the frustration of waiting. People with a lot of time on their hands and not much to do can easily become depressed and feel worthless.

  Talk about your experience with people whose lives revolve around waiting in some way. Do you have any friends, neighbors, or relatives in this category? Is their waiting temporary because of a particular situation, or will their experience of waiting continue until they die? How can you be part of their support system? What might some of their needs be? How can you respond to the advice: Don't just do something! Stand there!

- Be a friend. Listen to what your friends say about their parents, children, siblings, and other relatives. If someone in their family has had an accident, is suffering from an illness, is in prison, or has special needs, be willing to hear how life is for that person. Don't appear to be disinterested or uncomfortable about talking. Someone you know might be reluctant to discuss such situations for fear of grossing out or freaking out you or your friends. Such situations really aren't gross or freaky. They happen—they're part of life. When someone is trying to express how such painful waiting feels, we need to listen and not be judgmental. We need to be willing to take that advice: Don't just do something! Stand there!

- Let the symbols speak. Pay attention to time. Observe how often you check the time during the day. Notice how you spend your time. Are you too busy? Are you always rushing around without a break? Do you need a sabbath, a time of rest?

- Note the reason for the season. Lent is a time of sand—sand on the desert, sand in an hourglass. It's a time for crying out, "How long, O Lord?" It's a time for patience, a time for thinking about how you spend your time, a time for giving up something, a time for doing something special, a time for letting the symbols speak.

Take Time to Pray

This prayer can work alone, with friends, or with teens and parents together.

THE CALL TO PRAYER

Find an hourglass or a stopwatch. Take a moment to get in touch with our loving creator, the author of all time.

GOD'S WORD

Read Phil 1.3–11. (Paul wrote the Letter to the Philippians while in prison—it's one of the four captivity epistles. The other three are Ephesians, Colossians, and Philemon.)

REFLECTION

Slow down. Slow down and think of all the time there is. Some people say they just don't have enough time. Too busy, too much to do, too many hassles in life, too much pressure, too much stress.

For some people, time stands still. The hours creep by. Waiting is all they know. There are twenty-four hours in a day. The earth keeps spinning, as it always has, at about the same rate, year after year.

Moses lived through about twenty-four hours every day. So did the Israelite slaves in Egypt. So did the slaves who were kidnapped from Africa and sold to the plantation owners in our country's southern colonies and states. So did Jesus. So did Saint Paul.

Time is a gift. Give thanks for the time you have.

BLESSING

Watch the sand granules slip through the hourglass, or the second hand on the stopwatch tick away the seconds, for three full minutes. Hold up the hourglass or stopwatch with one hand, as if presenting the timepiece to God. Hold up your other hand, outstretched to God. Pray aloud the following words:

Creator, God, author of time, bless the hours and minutes we spend on earth. Help us to live well, work well, rest well, and love well during all of those blessed hours and minutes. Help us to spend some special time doing something we enjoy with someone who loves us. Amen.

CHAPTER 4

Why Do We Die?

Real Life

"Why are we planting these seeds here?"

Her little brother's question was innocent enough. After all, he was only six. How could he understand life and death, suffering and resurrection?

"We are planting them because they came from Grandma's tomatoes. You remember Grandma's garden? On the side of her house? That's where we used to pick all of our tomatoes. Do you remember that garden, Tony?"

"I remember. We have a picture of us with the big tomato plants. They're bigger than me!"

"Bigger than *I*."

"They're not that big!"

Never mind, Gina thought. Why correct a six-year-old's grammar? That's his teacher's job. Come to think of it, my teachers weren't the ones who taught me correct grammar. Our grandmother was. God, how we miss her.

"But didn't Grandma's tomatoes grow outside?"

"Yes, they did. But it's too cold to plant these seeds outside now. They would die. Plants need to stay warm."

"So we keep them in these little cups until it's warm outside?"

"Yes. When it gets warm, they'll be bigger. Then we'll transplant the seedlings into pots and plant the pots outside, and they'll grow into large tomato plants."

"When do we get tomatoes?"

"By the middle or end of the summer."

"Then they will be like Grandma's tomatoes?"

"I hope so. Do you remember Grandma? Let's go look at some pictures of you and Grandma."

They turned the pages and pointed out all the pictures of Grandma—Grandma in the garden, Grandma slicing tomatoes and making salad, Grandma sitting on the couch. In one of the older photo albums, they found pictures of Grandma and Grandpa. "Who's this?" Tony asked.

"That's Grandpa. You never met Grandpa. He died before you were born."

"Why do some people die, Gina?"

"Everyone dies, Tony. Grandma and Grandpa lived a long time, and when it was time for their life on earth to be over, they died."

"And now they live in heaven with God, but we can't see them yet, right?"

"Right. And when we pray they hear our prayers. And they keep loving us. I think they watched us plant the tomato seeds today."

Gina's mind drifted as they looked at the pictures. Grandma adored Tony, she thought, and he hardly got a chance to know her. She taught him how to write his name. He was only five when she died—when he went into her room to say good morning, and she wouldn't wake up.

Then the wake and the funeral. It was so hard for Tony to understand. Grandma looked as if she were sleeping. He just wanted to wake her up.

The rest of the summer, we kept going to Grandma's to get her tomatoes. We ate tomatoes every day. On sandwiches, in salads, as snacks. We tried to make her tomato sauce, but we could never get it to taste quite like hers.

One month from the day she died, we ate the last of her tomato sauce, defrosted from the freezer. Pasta would never taste like that again. In my mind, I can remember that taste; it's part of me now.

Will Grandma be part of Tony? Will Tony ever understand the deep connection between her life and his life? Gina hoped so.

"Is this one of Grandma's tomatoes?"

"Yes, that's the tomato that our seeds came from. We picked that tomato from Grandma's garden. We took the picture so we would remember it."

"And here's a picture of the seeds from the tomato?"

"That's right. And where are those seeds now?"

"In the little cups in the sunroom. When they start to grow, will we take more pictures of them?"

"Yes, we will. And then they'll grow bigger and bigger, until they have tomatoes on them."

"And then we can eat the tomatoes, right?"

"That's right."

"This tomato in the picture is gone now. But we can remember it."

"Right."

"That's like Grandma. Grandma's gone, too, but we can remember her."

"That's right, Tony. We can remember her with our pictures, and our memories."

"And with her tomatoes that keep growing from her seeds."

Gina felt better, in a strange sort of way. Tony did understand. She couldn't explain how, but she knew he did. It's something we learn as children and keep learning all our lives, yet still can't say how we know: Death leads to life. With people, with tomatoes, death leads to life.

A Closer Look

Why do we die? Why do we suffer?

Why is there evil in the world? Why do people even believe in God? God can do anything, so why doesn't God use almighty power to prevent people from doing evil? In fact, why doesn't God force everyone to be loving and kind and to do just the things that God and all good people want?

Perhaps this analogy will help: Think of God as a loving parent. Then, think of yourself as a parent. Picture yourself with a newly born baby. Let's imagine that modern science has developed a small device that could be surgically implanted in your baby's brain. This device would guarantee that your baby would always love you and would always do what you wanted, for as long as he or she lived. Would you want your child to have that implant? Probably not.

You probably would not want your child to have that implant because it would take away your child's capacity to really love you, and your opportunity to really be loved by your child. Love is a choice. Love is a decision. The implant would prevent your child from making that choice.

As a parent you would always wonder, Does my child really love me, or is it the brain device? Anything your child said or did wouldn't really count. You'd want to know that your child had chosen to love you, not just that he or she had been programmed to love you.

What good is forced love? It is not love at all. It's far better to be free to love. Nothing is better than really loving and being loved!

So in a way, this example can help us understand why God doesn't *force* us to be good and loving to everyone. God wants us to know real, true, honest love that comes from deep within ourselves.

The problem with having the freedom to love is obvious. We also have the freedom not to love, the freedom to hurt, the freedom to sin. So how do we learn to love? How do we learn to understand others, to sympathize and have compassion, to almost feel another person's pain?

Part of learning to love comes from struggling through our own pain. Once we know what it's like to hurt, we get a clue about what it might be like for someone else to hurt. So our pain actually helps prepare us to be better at loving. All the bad stuff of life helps us get a better piece of the good stuff. We get to the good by struggling through the bad.

This whole sequence is what we call the paschal mystery. Getting to Easter Sunday by going through Good Friday. It's the only way—the way of Jesus, the way of the cross. That's why Jesus tells us he is "the way, and the truth, and the life" (Jn 14.6–7).

So, does this mean that causing suffering is good? Does this mean that God causes us to suffer on purpose, because it's good for us and we can learn from it? Does this mean that loving parents should purposely bring suffering to their children in order to help them develop sympathy and compassion?

No, no, and no! God does not send us pain on purpose to teach us a lesson. Parents do not help their children by causing them to suffer, and we certainly do not help the world by deliberately causing pain!

Pain itself does not teach us; our struggle through the pain teaches us. Trying to shield a child from every possible disappointment is a wonderful recipe for creating a spoiled brat who doesn't care about the pain or needs of others, yet wants everyone's sympathy and attention.

God doesn't send us pain, but God does not shield us from every pain either. God stays with us when pain naturally happens and helps us come to grips with it, accept it, and grow through it. What God does with pain and hurt is also what good friends and good parents try to do.

The glory comes after the pain is finished. The resurrection comes after the crucifixion is over. Life comes after death.

In the Bible

The most painful suffering of all is the suffering caused by sin. That's the suffering Jesus endured.

A question often asked is, Why did Jesus have to suffer and die? Did Jesus suffer and die because God was so angry with all of us humans for being so sinful, that God had to punish someone? Did Jesus suffer and die because God needed to take revenge on somebody, and Jesus came forward as our substitute to endure the suffering we truly deserve? Did Jesus suffer and die because we needed a physical reminder of how horrible our sinfulness is, and God wanted us to feel guilty every time we looked at a crucifix?

No, no, and no! Because we are human beings, we die. Jesus died because he was human as well as divine. Jesus was born as one like us, so dying had to be part of Jesus' human experience.

Because we are human beings to whom God gives the freedom to love, we also have the freedom to sin. Jesus suffered a torturous death by crucifixion because some angry and jealous leaders used their political power sinfully. Like us, those leaders were human beings. Humans make mistakes. Humans are jealous. Humans are afraid. Humans are greedy. Humans sin and cause the most hurtful kind of pain.

At the same time, because we are human beings, we can recognize our sins, express our sorrow, ask for forgiveness, and seek ways to make things right again. God forgives us if we are truly sorry for our sins and the pain they cause, and God then allows that pain to become part of the paschal mystery of getting to the good by struggling through the bad.

Because we are human, we also suffer pain caused by the sins of others, just like Jesus did. But Jesus gave us the perfect example of compassion and forgiveness even in the midst of his own painful suffering. This is especially clear in Luke's Gospel (chapters 22–24).

Notice how strongly Jesus' anguish and pain is described as he prays on the Mount of Olives: "His sweat became like great drops of blood falling down" (22.44).

When the crowd comes to arrest Jesus, one of the Apostles tries to defend him and strikes the slave of the high priest, cutting off his ear. Notice that rather than thanking the Apostle, Jesus heals the slave's ear (see verse 51).

At the Last Supper, Jesus says, "I tell you, Peter, the cock will not crow this day, until you have denied three times that you know me" (verse 34). After the third time Peter denies Jesus, the cock crows. Notice that Jesus looks at Peter at that moment, most probably in compassion (see verse 61).

After Jesus has been sentenced to death, he follows Simon of Cyrene, who is carrying the cross. Notice that Jesus stops to comfort the women who are crying over his suffering (see 23.27–31).

After Jesus is hung on the cross between two thieves, he forgives his murderers (see verse 34). One of the thieves mocks Jesus. The other one criticizes the mocking thief and seeks comfort from Jesus. Notice that Jesus forgives him and promises him that they will meet soon again in Paradise (see verses 39–43).

Check It Out

The story of the Passion, death, and Resurrection of Jesus is told in all four Gospels. You can choose a different Gospel each day and spend some time reading that particular account from start to finish.

The *CYB* contains many other passages and articles relating to sin and salvation, reconciliation, the paschal mystery of death and new life, life after death, and the symbolism of sowing seeds. Check out the following Scripture passages as you explore those themes more deeply:

SEEDS

- unless a grain of wheat dies (Jn 12.24)
- the mustard seed (Mt 13.31–32, Mk 4.30–32, Lk 13.18–19)
- the sower (Mt 13.19; Matthew, chapters 18–23; Mk 4.1–9; Mark, chapters 13–20; Lk 8.4–8; Luke, chapters 11–15)
- the weeds and the wheat (Mt 13.24–30)
- the growing seed (Mk 4.26–29)

RECONCILIATION AND FORGIVENESS

- Joseph and his brothers (Genesis, chapter 45)
- David's sin (2 Sam 11.12–18)
- Jonah and Nineveh (Jonah)
- Forgive seventy-seven times. (Mt 18.21–22)
- the unforgiving servant (Mt 18.23–35)
- a sinful woman forgiven (Lk 7.36–50)
- the prodigal son (Lk 15.11–52)

- forgiving sins (Jn 20.21–23)
- "Feed my lambs." (Jn 21.15–19)

SUFFERING SERVANT SONGS

- bringing justice (Isa 42.1)
- "My cause is with the Lord." (Isa 49.1–6)
- "The Lord GOD helps me." (Isa 50.4–9)
- "He bore the sin of many." (Isa 52.13—53.12)

SIN AND SALVATION

- the tower of Babel (Gen 11.1–9)
- Abram and Sarai (Genesis, chapter 12)
- the golden calf (Exodus, chapter 32)
- introduction to the Book of Leviticus (page 107 of the *CYB*)
- the scapegoat (Lev 16.20–22)
- Deborah (Judges, chapters 4–5)
- resurrection (Dan 12.2)
- the paschal mystery (Rom 6.1–8)

What Next?

What can teenagers and parents do together to further explore the themes of sin and salvation, reconciliation, the paschal mystery, life after death, and the symbolism of sowing seeds. Here are some starter ideas for you:

- Discuss the Scriptures. For example, look up Jn 12.24–25 and the article "Dying for New Life," on page 1265 of the *CYB*. When has the loss of something you really wanted or thought you wanted turned into something wonderful you never expected? When did your painful goodbye to a bad situation turn into a glorious hello to another situation? The paschal mystery doesn't only refer to the physical death of your body at the end of your life and the rising of your soul to heaven; it also refers to every "emotional death" or suffering and its eventual "emotional resurrection" or related comeback. What are examples of emotional deaths and resurrections in your life?

- Discuss the story at the beginning of this chapter. What kind of understanding do you think a five-year-old boy like Tony could have of the paschal mystery and life after death? How might his understanding of life after death be different from yours or from that of his older sister, Gina? What experiences do you have with gardening or farming? When in your life have you planted seeds or watched seeds grow and blossom?

- Take a look at a difficult issue: People die every day. Some die young and suddenly, and some die after a long, full life. Usually when a person dies, someone in her or his family makes arrangements at a funeral home.

   Consider visiting a funeral home and taking a tour. Ask to see the coffins. Ask to see the room where they embalm bodies. Ask about the whole process of preparing a body for burial. Sooner or later, most people need to make funeral arrangements. It will be a lot less shocking for you if you're already familiar with what funeral homes are like behind the scenes.

- Be a friend. Don't miss an opportunity to apologize when you have hurt someone and need to make things right again. Be brave enough to go through the Good Fridays of reconciliation in order to reach the Easter Sundays of renewed friendship.

   Give extra time and attention to anyone who has had a family member or friend die recently. Don't be afraid to talk about death or heaven. Lots of people wonder about it, and sometimes it's hard to discuss because people's reactions to such talk might not be positive.

   Live well. Develop your interests and talents. Cultivate your friendships. The best preparation for a good and happy death is a good and happy life. Think of how you'd want people to describe you once you have died, and spend the rest of your life trying to become that person.

- Let the symbols speak. Pay attention to death and new life as they take place all around you in nature. Notice the change of the seasons. Note when something good dies out, when something else very good is born. Observe seeds being planted all around.

- Note the reason for the season. Halloween, All Saints' Day, and All Souls' Day are key times for honoring those who have died. The Triduum, which begins with Mass on Holy Thursday and ends with Easter, is the holiest season of all. It celebrates the paschal mystery, the dying and rising of Jesus the Christ.

Take Time to Pray

This prayer can work alone, with friends, or with teens and parents.

THE CALL TO PRAYER

Slice a tomato in half. Take a moment to get in touch with Jesus, who has suffered, died, and risen to new life.

GOD'S WORD

Read Lk 12.13–21.

REFLECTION

We never know which day will be our last. But we know our days are numbered. How will we choose to live? By trying to have everything we want, or by trying to want everything we have?

If we are always trying to find ways to have more and buy more and get more, then we will never have enough. We will always be dissatisfied. We will never have all we want. Our pride and greed will take over our life.

But if we are always trying to find ways to appreciate more and enjoy more and be satisfied with what we do have, then we will always have enough. We will always be satisfied. We will always want what we have.

Life is too short. At the moment of our death, what will matter the most to us? How much *stuff* we had during our life, or how much *love* we had during our life? Better that we live with forgiveness than with pride and greed. The rich man in the parable in Luke was indeed a fool. With all his wealth, he died very poor. Possessions cannot bring the happiness that comes with love.

Some people don't learn this lesson until death. When we die, the most valuable thing we leave behind is the seeds we sow. Often we are not around to see our own seeds blossom, but those who come after us enjoy that.

If we sow seeds of bitterness and stubbornness and criticism, that is what will grow in the loved ones we leave behind. If we sow seeds of love and forgiveness and compassion, that is what will grow in the loved ones we leave behind.

What kind of seeds are you sowing? What will grow when you leave this world behind?

BLESSING

Look at the seeds inside the tomato. Hold up the halves of the tomato as an offering to Jesus. Ask Jesus to bless the tomato seeds and all they represent. Ask Jesus to help you do your best to plant seeds of love and forgiveness. Ask Jesus to be with you throughout all your Good Friday times so you might struggle through and arrive at your Easter Sunday times. Eat the tomato and savor its flavor. Be grateful for everyone who plants seeds so that we might enjoy the fruits.

CHAPTER 5

How Do We Make a Comeback?

Real Life

Luke Christianson
English Honors Class

The Person I Most Admire

I was hanging out with my friends in the school parking lot. She came over, introduced herself, and gave us her card. Lynn Kelogi. She was the new youth minister at Holy Spirit. I told her I went to Holy Spirit.

"Great! I hope you'll join our youth leadership team," she said.

"What's a youth leadership team?" I asked.

"It's a special team of young people who want to make a difference in their church and in their community. A team who is willing to dream dreams, solve problems, make mistakes, learn from one another, work with some caring adults, and make the world a better place. Are you interested?"

"Maybe," I said. Her smile was something else—as if she already knew me.

"What's your name?" she asked.

"Luke," I told her.

"Luke, why don't you come to the ten o'clock mass this weekend and stay for a meeting? I'm inviting youth and adults interested in youth ministry at Holy Spirit. Free pizza. What have you got to lose? Bring some of your friends."

So I went to Mass that Sunday. I brought some of my friends. That way, I didn't have to sit with my parents. I was only a ninth grader that fall. I never did anything religious. I wasn't big on church. I believed in God, but I thought church stuff was boring. Well, it was until Lynn came along.

Three years later, our church was a different church. A youth choir took its turn singing at the ten o'clock mass every month. I became a lector. The boring classes were gone. Adults hosted youth groups in homes and other places. One group met at Pizza Hut, another group rotated homes to get more parents involved.

But the best part was the youth leadership team. We did all kinds of things. We had a leadership training retreat every year and we learned a lot—communication skills, group dynamics, problem-solving skills, decision-making skills, presentation skills, small-group facilitation skills, and leadership skills.

We came up with our own projects. We repainted all the rooms in the church basement and found ways to get the paint and brushes donated. We raised money so that we could attend leadership camp. We gave workshops for middle school kids in other churches in our area. We visited the hospice, and began building relationships with the different people who had come there to die. We painted bright, wonderful murals all over the walls there to make them less dreary. Our artwork was great! We began a special monthly prayer meeting. We read the Bible, talked about our problems, and discussed how we saw God working in our lives.

I became a new person. Lynn had brought about so many changes. She really believed in us, and she trained us, and she trained the adults in the parish to let us run things with their assistance. She called it youth empowerment.

Then Lynn's husband got transferred, and she had to move. It was the end of my junior year. We all thought we were going to die without her. We had huge a party, and all of us were crying by the time it was over. The parents loved her, the kids loved her, the parish staff loved her. She kept saying: "It's not me! Y'all are the ones who are special! Look at the wonderful projects y'all have started here in this parish!" She was so humble.

Then the week after we said good-bye to Lynn, we heard that our pastor would be leaving us as well. Our new pastor had never worked with a youth minister. He didn't think youth ministers were necessary. So he decided not to hire anyone at all. We were stunned. We thought everything we had built up would fall apart. We didn't have anyone to lead us, or teach us, or guide us. How could we keep all of this going?

Well, our parents were not going to let everything end for the youth. They got organized and decided that things would continue—with or without a new youth minister. It wasn't easy, but we did it. Our youth leadership team kept doing prayer meetings and service projects. Scheduling became more tricky, but by then I was a senior, and I took on lots of the organizational chores of the group myself.

All the adults really pitched in. Lynn had taught us well. Not only did she believe in youth empowerment, but she also believed in adult empowerment. We all had so much spirit that we believed we could do anything, whether or not the pastor was behind our efforts.

Then the youth leadership team put together a presentation for the parish council, on everything Lynn had started. We identified all the different areas of ministry we wanted to continue, and we proposed that the parish hire two youth ministers—one for high school teens and one for middle school teens. The council voted in favor of our proposal, and it has begun the hiring process.

Lynn left about eight months ago, and I'll be graduating soon. I know I won't be a member of the youth leadership team much longer, but I am glad the team will be in good hands. I'm proud that our whole parish pulled together to keep its youth ministry going. But most of all, I'm proud that it was the effort of teenagers that convinced the parish council to hire two youth ministers even though the pastor wasn't in favor of it at first.

I admire Lynn because she told us we could dream our dreams and make them come true. And because she taught us that if we work together, we can accomplish more than if we work separately. But most of all, I admire Lynn because she lived her life being true to the words she spoke. She couldn't do everything, and she didn't try to. She wasn't perfect, and she didn't need to be. She basically believed in people, and she encouraged us and taught us and celebrated who we are and what we had accomplished. Because of her example, I have decided to pursue studies in the field of ministry. I want to be able to bring other teenagers to a fuller faith life and a deeper commitment to faith community, the way she did at our parish.

A Closer Look

How do we recover once we are down? How do we make a comeback once we are behind? Where do we get the courage and energy? How do we get going again?

The world is not an easy place to live. Everything is not always wonderful. Sometimes we get hurt. Sometimes we are devastated. Bad things can happen to good people.

So when things are suddenly not going well anymore, what do we do? Do we curl up in a ball, curse God and the whole world, and stop trying? Sometimes we might do that, at least for a little while. But after we get past the shock, after we get past the anger, after we get past the sadness, what do we do?

Somehow we decide that it's time. We realize that life is for living and that it's not our time to die yet. So we become determined, and we start living again.

Is it easy? No, of course not. It's painful, frustrating, and exhausting. But somehow we do it. It takes courage and determination. It takes hope and faith. It takes the Holy Spirit.

And what is the Holy Spirit? The Holy Spirit is the part of God that lives within us. Deep down in our soul, the Holy Spirit drives us.

In Hebrew the word *ruah* has several meanings: "breath," "wind," and "spirit." When the world was first being created, "a wind from God swept over the face of the waters" (Gen 1.2).

When God was creating Adam, God "breathed into his nostrils the breath of life; and the man became a living being" (2.7).

Wind. Breath. Spirit. Ruah. Think of a wind sock. Or even a pinwheel, or wind chimes. You can't see the air moving through them, but its effects are obvious. Imagine a huge power plant harnessing the energy of the wind. Picture windmills turning and the movement being converted into electricity.

That's the Holy Spirit in our lives. A source of power. We can ignore it, waste the potential, and forget it's there. Or we can tap into it, get caught up in its movement, and accompany God to the holy places to which God takes us.

Certainly you have heard the words *discipleship* and *mission*. Those who followed Jesus were his disciples. They learned the ways of the Master directly. Those of us who follow Jesus today are also disciples.

Discipleship is the ongoing process of discovering the deeper meaning of our commitment to follow Jesus. It is also our lifelong journey to learn how to keep doing it better and better. Mission is the work of the followers of Jesus. It's the work of the church.

These words are difficult to explain in one sentence, but the Bible can help. The prophet Micah tells us what God requires of us: "To do justice, and to love kindness, and to walk humbly with your God" (Mic 6.8). When God is asked what the greatest commandment is, God says: "You shall love the LORD your God with all your heart, and with all your soul, and with all your might" (Deut 6.5). Very much like this greatest commandment is the second greatest commandment: "You shall love your neighbor as yourself" (Mt 22.34–40; see also Mk 12.28–34, Lk 10.25–28).

The Bible is filled with stories that illustrate what discipleship is, and what our mission is. Maybe you have seen the T-shirts and bumper stickers that read, "B.I.B.L.E. stands for Basic Instructions Before Leaving Earth!"

How are we supposed to be disciples? How do we know what our mission is? We need to be open to the guidance of the Holy Spirit. It is like looking at a wind sock to find out which direction the wind is blowing. Naturally, some situations are more confusing. At times we're caught in a storm, and we have difficulty reading the signs. The wind sock is blowing all over the place!

But the sin isn't in reading the wind incorrectly. The sin is deciding to ignore the wind, to not use the windsock at all.

In the Bible

The author of Luke's Gospel is also the author of the Acts of the Apostles. The Gospel of Luke was dedicated to *Theophilus,* whose name means "lover of God" or "the one who loves God." So in a way, the Gospel is dedicated to you if you love God!

Acts 1.1–2 says, "In the first book, Theophilus, I wrote about all that Jesus did and taught from the beginning until the day when he was taken up to heaven." Once again, Luke seems to be writing to us directly!

Luke's Gospel ends with Jesus' Ascension into heaven; Acts begins with the Ascension. Jesus promised that the Holy Spirit would come: "You will receive power when the Holy Spirit has come upon you" (Acts 1.8). Then the disciples watched Jesus ascend: "When he had said this, as they were watching, he was lifted up, and a cloud took him out of their sight" (1.9).

Imagine how this must have felt! Those friends of Jesus had seen him preach and perform miracles for three years. They had come to believe that he was the Son of God. Then they watched him get into trouble with the authorities, and they saw him crucified, tortured to death. They had just about given up all hope, when his tomb was discovered empty. Then he appeared to them, back from the dead!

Then he was gone again! Ascended! Up and gone! They must have been in shock! Along came two people in white robes, asking what seemed to be a rather silly question: "Why do you stand looking up toward heaven?" (Acts 1.11). What would you have answered? You may have said something like: "What are you, kidding? Come on! Jesus just floated up into the sky! I'm stunned! I'm ready to freak out! What else am I supposed to do?"

Calmly, the ones in white robes (angels?) clarified the situation by telling the disciples that Jesus would be returning in the same way they saw him leave.

Then, soon after the Ascension, Pentecost was recorded (see 2.1–13). At the time the disciples were sitting in a house. Perhaps they were sitting in the same house described in Lk 24.36–43 and Jn 20.19–23. John mentions that the doors of the house were locked because the disciples were afraid. We can't know for sure, but perhaps the disciples were still afraid. Perhaps they were trying to figure out how to bounce back, how to recover from losing Jesus again. Either way, they were inside a house when it happened.

The Holy Spirit came with the rush of wind and tongues of fire. And suddenly all the disciples were speaking in different languages, and people from all over the world were able to understand them.

Talk about a comeback! Talk about a recovery! These disciples were ready to go! They were on a mission! And the rest of the Book of Acts—in fact, the rest of the New Testament—continues to tell their story! Powered by the Holy Spirit, the disciples thought they could do anything! And they were right!

Check It Out

The story of the Ascension and Pentecost is recorded most dramatically by Luke in the Acts of the Apostles. You can read Acts 1.1—2.24 to get the whole picture.

The Bible has other passages about mission and discipleship, about being called by God, about the Holy Spirit in general, and about Confirmation. The following lists present other Scripture passages and articles from the *CYB* that you might check out as you explore those themes more deeply:

WIND AND FIRE

- Creation (Gen 1.1–2; 2.7)
- God as a smoking torch (Gen 15.7–21)
- God as cloud by day and fire by night (Ex 13.21)
- Pentecost (Acts 2.1–13)

MISSION AND DISCIPLESHIP

- Samuel anointing David king (1 Sam 16.13)
- Ruth being faithful (Ruth)
- the cost of discipleship (Mk 4.18)
- Stephen martyred (Acts 7.51–61)
- discipleship as new life (Eph 5.1–20)
- Do not quench the Spirit. (2 Thess 5.16–19)
- rekindling the spirit of power (2 Timothy, chapters 6–7)
- the communal call to be models (1 Pet 2.9–17)

CALLED BY GOD

- Abraham (Gen 12.1–9)
- Moses (Ex 3.1—4.7)
- Samuel (1 Samuel, chapter 3)
- Israel (Isa 43.1–7)
- Jeremiah (Jer 1.4–10)
- Jesus' disciples (Mt 4.18–22)
- Mary (Lk 1.26–38)
- Paul (Acts 9.1–19)

THE HOLY SPIRIT IN GENERAL

- the spirit of God (Job 33.4)
- a new heart and spirit (Ezek 36.25–27)
- "Your sons and your daughters shall prophesy." (Joel 2.28)
- "She is a breath of the power of God." (Wis 7.24–30)
- gifts of the Spirit (Isa 61.1–2)
- fruits of the Spirit (Gal 5.22–26)

THE HOLY SPIRIT AS AN ENTITY THAT CANNOT BE CONTROLLED OR PREDICTED

- Jesus speaks to Nicodemus. (Jn 3.1–21)
- Joshua complains to Moses. (Num 11.24–30)
- John complains to Jesus. (Mk 9.38–41)
- The Holy Spirit is among the Gentiles. (Acts 10.44–48)

What Next?

What can teenagers and parents do together to further explore the themes of mission and discipleship, power of the Spirit, Confirmation, and Wind? Here are some starter ideas for you:

- Discuss the Scriptures. For example, read Lk 18.18–30 and 19.1–10. Compare and contrast the rich ruler and Zacchaeus. Use the articles "The Loaded Question" and "Noticed by Jesus," on pages 1231 and 1232 of the *CYB*, to help your conversation. When have you been like the rich ruler? When have you been like Zacchaeus? How hard would it be for you to unload some unnecessary possessions? What else is hard about being a radical follower of Jesus? Read Lk 9.1–6 and the article "Mission Possible," on page 1216 of the *CYB*. Is this kind of discipleship possible or impossible for you?

- Discuss the story at the beginning of this chapter. Luke Christianson, who has written an essay for English class, is a lot like the Luke who wrote the Gospel and the Acts of the Apostles. Both Lukes describe the leadership of someone who got a group of people fired up and then had to leave them behind. Both Lukes describe the Holy Spirit actively working with a group of believers that is trying to bounce back. Did you notice that similarity? What else did you notice? How can you be like the Lukes and involve yourself in such efforts by participating and even recording?

- Take a look at a difficult issue: All around you, people are trying to make a comeback. People are trying to recover from alcoholism, rape, divorce, mental depression, physical injury, illness, and disease. People are trying to recover from acne, embarrassment, breakups, and bad grades on tests.

  Discuss the kind of support offered by your family, school, parish, and community. If you needed special attention and assistance to recover from a traumatic situation, where would you go for help? Who are the people you trust? If someone came to you with a problem too big for you to help solve alone, where would you turn for guidance? The courage of the Holy Spirit is everywhere, moving us to take action, to be survivors, and to get going.

- Be a friend. When someone is recovering from a difficult situation, be sensitive and supportive. Share your gifts of courage and understanding. Share your strength. Share your wonder and awe. These are some of the gifts of the Holy Spirit. Keep your wind sock out in the wind so that you can figure out where the Holy Spirit is directing you to go.
- Let the symbols speak. Pay attention to the wind in your hair. Observe the wind blowing through the branches of trees. Realize that the Holy Spirit works like the wind. You can't see the Spirit, only the results. Decide to let the Spirit move you, so that you may in turn move others.
- Note the reason for the season. The Holy Spirit is the special focus of Ascension and Pentecost. Pentecost is often called the birthday of the church because the Spirit came to the gathered disciples and gave them the courage to become a true faith community.

Take Time to Pray

This prayer can work alone, with friends, or with teens and parents.

THE CALL TO PRAYER

Display a wind sock, pinwheel, or set of wind chimes. Take a moment to get in touch with the spirit of God.

GOD'S WORD

Read Lk 4.14–21.

REFLECTION

God has said: "The Spirit is upon you. The Spirit of God has anointed you. You have a mission. You are my disciple. You are to spread my Good News to everyone. Those who are struggling will no longer have to struggle. All will be set free from the chains that bind them. This is the year! This is the day! Now is the moment! Now is the time!

"You will tell everyone that now is the favored time of God! There is a lot of work to do, but you will do it. You are empowered by the Holy Spirit. Inhale deeply. Exhale deeply. Feel the power of the breath of God in your lungs! You will receive the gift of understanding! You will be giv-en knowledge and wisdom! You will be blessed with courage and good judgment, reverence and awe!

"These gifts of the Holy Spirit are yours! You are the one! You have the power! You are called! You are like Peter! like Paul! like Luke! You are called to live the story of Jesus with your very life! Go forth and bring my message of Good News to the world!"

BLESSING

Pray down the Holy Spirit onto your efforts. Stand up and take a deep breath. Feel the Spirit of God in your lungs. Extend your hands and reach up to the sky. Take another deep breath. Gently blow on your wind sock, pinwheel, or wind chimes. Take one last deep breath. Let the energy of ruah fill you. End the prayer by saying, "Come, Holy Spirit! Amen."

CHAPTER 6

What Are We Called to Be?

Real Life

Good morning!

I have never spoken at a school assembly before; in fact, I have never even given a speech before, but for some reason, I am not really very nervous. I want to tell you about what happened to me after I graduated from high school.

Two years ago, I had a lot of worries in my life. I worried about my family. What was the best way to lie to my parents and do what I wanted to do? How could I get to my friend's house and watch movies instead of going to the library? When I wanted money, what school supplies could I pretend I needed it for? Could I get away with it, or would my younger brother or sister find out, tattle, and get me into trouble?

I worried about my clothes. What kind of designer labels were in? Was everyone wearing shirts with collars, or were turtlenecks coming back? Was everyone still wearing sweatshirts inside out, or had they stopped that? What kinds of shoes should I get? The more expensive they were, the more status I would get by wearing them.

I worried about school. How could I look cool and hang around with all the cool kids? I wanted a friend with a car. I didn't want to take the bus like all the losers. I figured cute girls always went for the cool guys in the cool cars. That's all I was after.

When I was a senior, I didn't know what to do with my life. I never really cared about anyone but myself, so I wasn't even sad about leaving my so-called friends. But everyone was making plans. I didn't apply to any colleges, and I didn't know what kind of a job I wanted. Flunking out was beginning to sound like a good idea. At least people would stop asking me things like, "So, what are you doing after graduation?" I had no plans, and I was embarrassed to admit that.

So one day, a pretty nice looking girl asked me if I wanted to go away for a year with her on a vacation, all expenses paid. Sounds like quite an offer, huh? That's what I thought. I was so dense that I didn't even understand that she was talking about a church mission trip. She and I went to the same church, but I just never paid attention.

She assumed I knew what she was talking about because she once had half a conversation with me about this trip to Central America. I'm sure she told me what it was all about, but I'm equally sure that I never heard a word she said. So I agreed to go on this trip. A year in Guatemala and El Salvador. I had nothing else to do with my life. And it ended my "after graduation" dilemma.

Now when people asked what I planned to do after graduation, I could say, "Well, I'm going to travel for a year." Everyone was impressed by that—especially me. So I packed my bag, met this girl at the church, got on the bus, and headed to Central America.

Imagine my surprise when I learned that we were going to be living without air-conditioning and personal computers. Imagine my surprise when I learned that everyone on the trip was expected to be fluent in Spanish. What was I in for? *Muchas problemas*—that's what!

But I learned plenty of Spanish on this trip—and more. For one thing, I learned to pay attention. And I learned that people are basically the same—and amazingly different—in different parts of the world. I learned that most teenagers worry about the same things that I worried about in high school—more or less.

For example, like me, they worry about their families. Only they worry about whether or not they will see their relatives again. Many of the fathers and older brothers are kidnapped and forced to join the armies. People just disappear. Mothers and sisters keep their hopes alive by praying and talking to other families and passing along stories of sightings.

Like me, these teenagers also worry about clothes. Only they worry about how to clean their clothes after it rains. When it rains, all the water collects on the mud floor in the hut where they are sleeping, so when they wake up, their clothes are caked with mud. They then have to walk a mile to the river, where they can wash their clothes.

Like me, these teenagers also worry about school. Imagine a school with one roll of toilet paper on the teacher's desk! If you have to go out to use the bathroom, that means going to an outhouse, a seat over a hole in the ground, with half a curtain around it. You approach the teacher, ask for permission, and then receive your allotted four squares of toilet paper.

I never realized how selfish I had been until I realized how unselfish other people were. We visited a family that had one chicken and a small vegetable garden. Every day they ate vegetables, an egg, and maybe some bread if they could find some flour and oil. When we came to visit, they wanted to offer us their best hospitality. They killed their only chicken because they knew that people from the United States were accustomed to eating meat with every meal. They didn't even know us, and they killed their only chicken for us.

Well, I know you don't want to listen to me go on and on, so here's the deal: We got back from our trip about six months ago and put together some resources to share with schools. First, we'll watch a video here together, and then each class will have an opportunity to tour the resource room. It's set up in the library, with booklets, diaries, maps, and photo albums from the trip. We also brought back some crafts from El Salvador and Guatemala. I'll be coming to individual classrooms to answer questions and share some more stories.

Thank you for your attention so far, and now we'll watch the video.

A Closer Look

Isn't our world unbelievable? We have the technology to fly astronauts through space, to communicate instantly with others around the world, and to launch media campaigns that can persuade people how to dress, what to drive, and where to vacation.

In the United States, most families have several cars, televisions, radios, tape and CD players, computers, and other appliances. Yet worldwide, many children and adults have never even used a telephone.

Too many people in the world have too few resources. And too few people in the world have too many resources! How does this happen? How is it that in our new millennium, the world is more capable of solving the problem of world hunger, yet also more capable of destroying itself with global pollution or global war?

The rich get richer and the poor get poorer. Once a person or a country becomes rich, that person or country has the capability to abuse the power of money. Poor people and poor countries don't have status. No one listens to them. No one cares. It's easier to blame the poor for their poverty than it is to take some responsibility for it. After all, each individual person has such limited influence. How can you or I solve the world's problems? Besides that, there are a few very powerful people willing to do very inhuman things in order to gain or maintain political and economic control.

Is there no hope? The bad news is that not one of us can solve the world's problems. The good news is that not one of us is expected to. *All* of us are expected to.

If we are not part of the solution, then we are part of the problem. Each of us could say: "Hey! This is not my fault—I did nothing!" But people doing *nothing* is part of the problem. People doing *something* is part of the solution.

Consider this example: If you move into a clean apartment, and you do nothing to keep it clean, then it soon will be dirty. If you move into a clean apartment, and you do something every day to keep it clean, then it will stay clean, more or less.

Suppose you and four friends move into a dirty apartment. If three people do no cleaning, but you and one other person do some cleaning every day, then what will happen? The cleaners will be part of the solution, not part of the problem, and at least sections of the apartment will stay clean. And who knows? Perhaps the other three will see the difference and eventually begin to develop some cleaning habits because of your example.

The world can be compared to an apartment. One person can't keep it clean if four people are creating messes. Two people might be able to keep it clean but the work might be difficult. And if three people worked on it, the work would be easier.

Naturally the world is more complicated than an apartment with five friends. In the real world, not everyone is a friend. Everyone has different ideas of what *clean* is. Some people aren't capable of cleaning up after themselves. Some would be capable, but they don't have the tools or the knowledge. Some people have no idea they are making a mess, and they aren't open to learning about it. And some are rich and in control, with the power to direct the poor ones to clean the rich area, while the rest of the place gets poorer and dirtier.

Proverbs 21.13 says, "If you close your ear to the cry of the poor, you will cry out and not be heard." So what's our responsibility? We can't do everything, and we don't have to do everything. We just have to do *something*. Something extra. That's what justice is all about. It's not fair that I do extra work when someone else doesn't do any. It's also not fair that I was born into a family that owns a house with electricity and plumbing.

The world isn't fair. Justice goes beyond fairness. Justice is about *doing something extra* so that others who have too little might have a little more; *becoming more aware* of what's unfair in the world; *learning more* so that we can figure out how things became so unfair in the first place; *searching our heart* for our own personal values; and *sitting in the wisdom of the Scriptures* and our Catholic faith traditions. And when enough people start acting justly, the Spirit catches on. And once the Holy Spirit starts moving, there's no stopping it.

In the Bible

Matthew's Gospel has an extraordinary passage about our call to do justice (25.31–46). Jesus is telling his followers what it will be like at our final judgment. You will not be tested on the names of the Old Testament prophets or on the Ten Commandments. You will be judged by your acts of justice and mercy: Did you give a hungry, thirsty person some food and water? Did you welcome a stranger, a foreigner, a person of a different culture? Did you give a homeless or naked person some clothing? Did you visit a sick person or a prisoner? Or did you do nothing?

If you did nothing to help when you met someone in need, then you rejected a human being, and in doing so, you rejected Jesus. If you did something to help, then you helped Jesus—even if you couldn't solve the world's problems of hunger, thirst, hatred, poverty, disease, or crime.

Throughout all the Gospels, the words and actions of Jesus really point to one thing—taking care of the little ones. And this does not mean only children but it means all people whose importance is seen as too little to matter, such as homeless people, poor people, elderly people, sick people, prisoners—those who can't really repay you in money or physical resources.

What about the hungry man in Tanzania? Feed him. What about the thirsty girl in Haiti? Give her water. What about the new family with different colored skin in your neighborhood? Welcome them. What about the homeless man shivering in the streets? Give him clothing. What about the sick woman in India? Give her medicine and health care. What about the criminal in prison? Visit or write to him. What about all of them? Do you do it all? Do you go everywhere and do everything? No, of course not! You don't have to do everything! You just have to do *something*—something extra. But what if he smells? What if she keeps shouting or rambling or talking nonsense? What if you feel uncomfortable? What if they don't appreciate what you're doing? What if they try to take advantage of you?

Well, it's important to take care of yourself as well. Even Jesus took time to rest and get away from it all. Jesus didn't cure every blind, deaf, and sick person in all of Judea, but he made the rounds, and he welcomed and comforted, and he taught by his example so that others might begin to do the same. The spirit of Jesus is what beckons us to follow now.

You don't have to put yourself in danger or put others at risk, but you need to be prepared for a few disappointments, and maybe a few surprises. Every poor person you try to help won't be nice and sweet and grateful. Poverty hurts a person's spirit. Try to imagine what it would be like if you lost your job, your home, your way of life. You'd start to feel resentful and bitter. You'd be tired and crabby from walking around, and you'd be angry that other people still had jobs and homes and luxuries. Someone gives you a dollar? or a sandwich? Big deal! You're supposed to think they're something special? Why are they better than you? They're not! You're just as good. You're tired of being treated like an animal! You're a human being! You have feelings!

You get the picture. Be careful because some poor people will try to take advantage of you. After all, taking advantage of others is a form of survival. If you were starving, you might consider stealing some food in order to stay alive. See how the rules can change when people are desperate?

Every poor person you try to help might not need or want the kind of help you're ready to give. Often, the best way to help is just to listen. It's important to treat everyone as a human being, a son or daughter of God. That's what Jesus did. He ate with lepers and prostitutes. He socialized with tax collectors and other criminals and sinners. He let them become important to him; they became his friends. Sometimes the most powerful healing comes from simple caring.

Strange as it sounds, people in justice work often report that they have received more than they have given. Every person—even a hungry person or a homeless person or a sick person—has a story to tell and a lesson to teach. If we are willing to be humble servants of others, we may be surprised at what we come away with.

Funny how the spirit of justice works—the Holy Spirit of justice, that is! We start off trying to give, and we discover that we receive. We start off thinking that we can't do anything, and we discover that we can at least do something. Or we start off thinking that we don't need to do anything, and then we discover that we need to do so much. The Holy Spirit challenges us to be part of the solution rather than part of the problem.

Check It Out

The *CYB* has many passages and articles on the themes of social justice, human concerns, dignity of the person, and global issues. The ones in the following lists are some you might check out as you explore this theme more deeply:

JUSTICE IN THE PENTATEUCH (THE FIRST FIVE BOOKS OF THE BIBLE)

- the goodness and harmony of Creation (Gen 1.1—2.3)
- Jubilee and returning the wealth (Leviticus, chapter 25)
- our treatment of poor people, aliens, widows, and orphans (Deuteronomy, chapter 24)

JUSTICE IN THE HISTORY AND WISDOM BOOKS

- Esther and Mordecai (Esther)
- the song of justice (Psalm 82)
- the cry of the poor people (Prov 21.13)
- speaking out (Prov 31.8–9)

JUSTICE IN THE PROPHETS

- "the year of the Lord's favor" (Isa 61.1–2)
- worship without hypocrisy (Am 5.21–24)
- those who cheat the poor (Am 8.4–8)

JUSTICE IN THE GOSPELS

- loving your enemies (Mt 5.43–48)
- giving alms (Mt 6.2–4)
- welcoming the little ones (Mt 19.13–15)
- the final judgment (Mt 25.31–46)
- the greatest commandment (Mk 12.28–34)
- Mary's song (Lk 1.46–56)
- Blessed are you, woe to you. (Lk 6.20–26)
- the good Samaritan (Lk 10.29–37)
- the Pharisee's cup (Lk 11.37–42)

- the great dinner (Lk 14.7–24)
- the rich man and Lazarus (Lk 16.13–15)
- Who is the greatest? (Lk 22.24–27)
- a Samaritan woman at the well (Jn 4.1–30)
- a man born blind (John, chapter 9)

JUSTICE IN THE LETTERS

- generosity (2 Cor 8.13–14)
- faith and action (Jas 2.14–17)
- a warning to the rich (Jas 5.1–6)

What Next?

What can teenagers and parents do together in order to further explore the themes of social justice, human concerns, dignity of the person, and global issues? Here are some starter ideas for you:

- Discuss the Scriptures. For example, read Mt 25.31–46 and the article "You Did It to Me," on page 1159 of the *CYB*. Use questions like these to stimulate your conversation: What is your attitude toward the poor? What is your immediate reaction to this reading and all it implies? Have you ever served in a soup kitchen, built a home, gone on a mission trip, or written letters to someone in prison? What might you be willing to do together as a family?
- Discuss the story at the beginning of this chapter. What were you thinking and feeling as you read it? How might you have regarded this speaker had you met him during his senior year of high school? He sounds like he was shallow, disinterested in grades or colleges, without any ambition or life goals. Teens: Does he remind you of yourself or any of your friends? If so, how? Parents: Does he sound like the kind of friend you want your son or daughter to hang out with or date? Why or why not?

   Then look at the transformation he underwent! What do you think of the young man he has become? How has he changed? How does anyone change? Teens: Would you want to be his friend now? Why or why not? Parents: Would you want someone like him to influence your son or daughter? Why or why not?

- Take a look at a difficult issue: All over the country, and all over the world, poor people struggle. The rich get richer, and the poor get poorer. North America gobbles up more food and resources than any other continent. It really isn't enough just to give to the poor. It's also important to start challenging the structures that keep the poor in poverty and allow the rich to abuse with their wealth and power.

    A process called the pastoral circle is used by justice workers all over the world. It involves four stages, and the circle just keeps repeating itself. The process is outlined in the appendix of this book. Read it together, and ask yourselves this question: "How can the pastoral circle help us become part of the solution rather than part of the problem?"

- Be a friend. Remember that every poor person, every oppressed person, every person who is left out of the loop, every person you don't like, every person you haven't met yet, every person with different colored skin, every person of a different religion, every person from a different school or neighborhood or country is a child of God. The Spirit of God lives inside each of us, calls us to be people of justice, calls us to do something extra.

- Let the symbols speak. Pay attention. Realize we live in a global neighborhood, a multicultural church. Notice maps and globes and other reminders of all the different languages, music, foods, and customs of the world. Be open.

- Note the reason for the season. Justice is a strong theme throughout Lent and Advent, the two seasons of preparation in the liturgical year of the church. It is also a strong theme throughout the ordinary time of the church year.

Take Time to Pray

This prayer works very well when teenagers and parents pray it together. It can also work with one person alone or with a small group of friends.

THE CALL TO PRAYER

Look at a globe or a world map. Take a moment to get in touch with the spirit of poverty, the Holy Spirit of justice.

God's Word

Read Lk 16.19–31.

Reflection

Usually the names of those who are rich are the ones we remember. The names of those who are poor seem unimportant.

But in Jesus' story, only the poor person has a name. The rich man suffers for all eternity because he is not generous. Yet how many of us would tolerate a homeless person living at our gate or in our own backyard?

In this story the rich man is concerned about his whole family; he asks if Lazarus would return to earth to warn his rich brothers. Abraham assures him that even someone rising from the dead would not be convincing enough to change the habits of the rich and powerful. Has Jesus, the one who rose from the dead, changed our habits?

The world is filled with people like Lazarus. And quite a few of us are like the rich man. We are far from doomed. We have resources, and we have mercy, and we have been called to bring justice to the world.

We are called to awareness. We are called to action. We are called to reflection. We are called to analyze why there is injustice in the first place. The spirit of Jesus is calling us. It's time to respond.

Blessing

Spin the globe or look at the map. Close your eyes and point to a place. Open your eyes, see the country you have chosen, imagine the language, the dress, and the people living there. Do this a few times. Pray for the people each time. Pray for health and happiness, for fulfilling work, and for good friends. Ask the Spirit of God to bless the people of the world— every Lazarus, and every rich person—and to help all of us become stronger people of justice.

CHAPTER 7

Who Is God?

Real Life

Welcome to the Christian Youth Chat Room.

CatsupLeeJr has just entered the chat.

[xLuvsFIRE] I'M HAVING A BAD-HAIR DAY.
[CatsupLeeJr] Wuz up?
[SusieQ] Don't care about hair.
[xLuvsFIRE] @CATS: YOU LOVE KETCHUP OR WHAT?
[Grits2go] Type lkjlkj if you want to chat with me.
[CatsupLeeJr] Good guess.
[SusieQ] lkjlkjlkjlkjlkjlkjljklkjljlkjlkjlj

Shadow7 has just entered the chat.

[Grits2go] What's with the hair?

Faith has just entered the chat.

[SusieQ] Grits, are you from the South?
[Shadow7] Hi, Faith.
[Grits2go] @Q: Alabama. Roll Tide
[Faith] Hi, Shadow. 'sup?
[SusieQ] I was in Montgomery once
[xLuvsFIRE] WHO LIKES MUSTARD BETTER THAN KETCHUP?

Algebra has just entered the chat.

[Shadow7] I like your name, Faith. Do you like your faith?
[xLuvsFIRE] WHO LIKES MAYO BETTER THAN KETCHUP?
[Faith] Yup. God is awesome
[CatsupLeeJr] Who likes Catsup better than ketchup?
[Shadow7] I thought this was a Christian chat room
[Shadow7] Nobody's talking about God
[Grits2go] @Q: Where do you live?
[Faith] (private chat to Shadow7) pc me and we can talk about God
[SusieQ] Nebraska. Go Big Red

CatsupLeeJr has just left the chat.

[Grits2go] @Q: Age/sex? For real

[Shadow7] (private chat to Faith) Do you pray?

[SusieQ] 16/f. Now you tell me yours

[Faith] (private chat to Shadow7) Every day. God's awesome. He helps me. I was with my grandfather when he died. I felt God for sure.

[Grits2go] 17/m

[xLuvsFIRE] WHO LIKES GRITS BETTER THAN ALGEBRA?

[Algebra] Fire: Stop YELLING at us!

[Shadow7] (private chat to Faith) I may be weird, but I don't think of God as a "he" cuz God's a spirit. So no body, no gender

[xLuvsFIRE] STOP IGNORING ME!

[Faith] (private chat to Shadow7) You're not weird. Nobody knows what God looks like. You're right. He's a spirit

[Algebra] Hey, I'm not ignoring you

[Shadow7] (private chat to Faith) HE'S a Spirit??? Why not SHE?

[xLuvsFIRE] @Algebra: DO YOU LIKE MATH OR SOMETHING?

[Faith] Who thinks God is male? Who thinks God has no gender?

[Algebra] Algebra

[xLuvsFIRE] GOD DOESN'T HAVE SEX.

[SusieQ] Just people have sex. That's how we all got here

[Algebra] If God doesn't want sex, I'll take it. Who else wants sex?

[Grits2go] @Algebra: This is a Christian chat room. Obey the rules or we all click ignore on you.

[xLuvsFIRE] WHO CARES? GOD IS GOD!

[Grits2go] The Bible says God is a man. Jesus' Father.

[Faith] At church, we always call God Father, but maybe we shouldn't. Maybe she's a spirit, like the Holy Spirit, and Shadow's right.

[Shadow7] Bible says having slaves is okay, too. So is having many wives. Gotta be careful with "Bible says so."

[SusieQ] I thought the Bible was the word of God. How can we disagree?

[xLuvsFIRE] OUR FATHER WHO ART IN HEAVEN. END OF DISCUSSION.

[Faith] The Bible was inspired by God, but written by men who lived in a culture that favored men.

[xLuvsFIRE] OUR FATHER WHO ART IN HEAVEN. END OF DISCUSSION.

[Shadow7] I think you have to understand the culture of Bible times. Women used to be property. No wonder men wrote the Bible that way.

[Grits2go] So, what, now God made a mistake?

[SusieQ] Can you change what the Bible says? Isn't that like a sin?

[Grits2go] You expect me to pray to a lady God?

[Shadow7] We just don't have a word that means HE OR SHE person. IT doesn't mean a person. IT means a thing. So it's hard to describe God as a person without making God a he or a she.

xLuvsFIRE has just left the chat.

[Faith] If God has to be a male to be important, then that means males are more important than females. I thought we were beyond that.

[Shadow7] What's wrong with praying to God and thinking female? If God has no body and no gender, then why is it okay to say HE and not okay to say SHE?

[Algebra] This makes sense

[SusieQ] I never think of God like this

[Shadow7] It's not supposed to be easy to understand. God is a mystery.

[Faith] Ever think about the Trinity? That's even harder to think about! Three persons, one God.

[SusieQ] So you believe what you don't understand?

[Grits2go] FATHER, SON, and Holy Spirit

[Algebra] The Holy Spirit's female?

[Shadow7] Try Parent, Jesus, and Spirit. Try Parent, Offspring, and Spirit. Try Almighty, Eternal Word, and Divine Spirit.

[Grits2go] FATHER, SON, and Holy Spirit

[Faith] Try Yahweh, Jesus, and Sophia!

[Grits2go] Try something else

Grits2go has just left the chat.

[Faith] (private chat to Shadow7) This was not a good idea. Sorry.

[SusieQ] God has no body. I get that. It's this male-female thing. . . .

[Shadow7] (private chat to Faith) It's okay. Thanks for trying. What's your e-mail address? Mine is sbooker@aul.con. I'll e-mail you.

[Algebra] And I thought calculus was blowing my mind!

[Faith] (private chat to Shadow7) Good idea. Faith@kydso.met. Bye!

She-God has just entered the chat.

Shadow7 has just left the chat.

Faith has just left the chat.

[She-God] Was it something I said?

A Closer Look

God is mysterious, isn't he? Or, rather, isn't she? Umm . . . isn't God? It's difficult to talk about God and image a person without thinking of one gender or another. A lot of people struggle with this issue. The Bible has different images of God. Some are definitely male, such as Lord and Father. But some are female, such as these:

- mother (see Num 11.12–13)
- mother eagle (see Deut 32.11–12)
- mother bear (see Hos 13.8)
- mother hen (see Mt 23.37)
- woman (see Lk 15.8–10)

Some have no gender at all, such as these:

- rock (see Ps 18.2)
- light (see Ps 27.1)
- potter (see Isa 64.8)

And yet so many people are much more comfortable calling God Father. Why is that? Well, for most of the church's history, society saw men as superior to women; in fact, women and children were considered the property of men. Men were in charge; men wrote the books. It's astonishing that even one female image of God appeared in such a culture. But lots of them did.

God has no body. God has no gender. Any sense of being a male is simply something people have gotten used to. When referring to God, it's just as accurate to say "she" as it is to say "he."

What else do we know about God? We know that when God was revealed to Abraham, God's name, YWHW, was never spoken. It was too holy to say aloud. When people asked Moses to name the God who sent him, he was told to call God "I Am Who I Am." The Hebrews and the Israelites of the Old Testament didn't know of Jesus. They knew only of the Almighty One. They knew only of their Creator.

Later on, when the disciples began to understand who Jesus was, they realized that he was the messiah, their savior and redeemer. They began to understand the Holy Spirit, who was their helper, the one who brought them healing power, the one who sanctified them and made all holy.

So does that mean that YHWH is the creator, and that Jesus is the redeemer, and that the Holy Spirit is the sanctifier? Well, that might be the way the Trinity has been revealed to us throughout history, but it's not that simple. God as Trinity means that there is one God made of three divine persons with different relationships to one another. So God creates, God redeems, God makes holy—all together, all one God, all three persons.

But doesn't Jesus talk to Abba (another name for YWHW; see Mk 14.36, Rom 8.15, Gal 4.6)? And doesn't Jesus promise to send the Holy Spirit? Yes. So does it all make sense? Of course not! We can't possibly understand God—we can only come close to describing God with images and analogies and creative stories. We cannot explain God. God is a mystery. Yet somehow, we receive the gift of faith, and we believe.

In the Bible

Isaiah has a tender message of love from God. The people feel forgotten and abandoned by God. They are captives in a strange land and are having doubts about God. God tells them of her love for them:

> Can a woman forget her nursing child,
>> or show no compassion for the child of her womb?
> Even these may forget,
>> yet I will not forget you.
> See, I have inscribed you on the palms of my hands.

(Verses 15–16)

God gives them hope:

> Lift up your eyes all around and see;
>> they all gather, they come to you.

As I live, says the LORD,
> you shall put all of them on like an ornament,
> and like a bride you shall bind them on.

(Isa 49.18)

Despite the masculine word LORD in the middle of this section, the overall images are feminine. God is a tender, gentle, loving parent who cradles us and softly reassures us that she is still here with us. Hush now. Do not fret. All of your worries and troubles will not harm you. The day will come when you will wear them like jewels on your bridal day.

If you read the article "I Will Never Forget You, My People," on page 873 of the *CYB*, you will note that the Hebrew root of the word *compassion* means "womb." A God of compassion is a God who loves you as a mother cherishes the precious child in her own womb. This female image of God gives new meaning to the words we hear every Sunday at the Eucharist: "This is my body, this is my blood."

You may feel uncomfortable stretching your image of God to include the feminine; that's a natural and typical response. Don't worry about it, but do try getting over it. It might not be a bad idea to image God differently the next time you pray. Once you start using more imagination with your prayer life, you will greatly enhance your relationship with our God, who is much too huge to be confined to just one image.

Check It Out

On page 1086 of the *CYB* is the article "Images of God." The *CYB* actually has many articles about God's revelation and how God's revelation has come to us. The following are some Scripture passages you might check out as you explore this theme more deeply:

- God as creator (Genesis, chapter 1)
- God of ancestors (Ex 3.13–15)
- holy God (Lev 11.44–45)
- God as warrior (Deuteronomy, chapter 20)
- God as mystery (Job 42.1–5)
- God of poor people (Psalm 12.5)
- God as shepherd (Ps 23)
- God as potter (Jer 18.1–6)
- universal God (Jonah)

- God as wisdom (Wis 6.12–20)
- God as just judge (Mt 25.31–46)
- God as father (Lk 11.12)
- God as housewife (Lk 15.8–10)
- Jesus as Word of God (Jn 1.1–18)
- God as love (1 Corinthians, chapter 13)
- Jesus as image of God (Col 1.15–20)

What Next?

What can teenagers and parents do together in order to further explore the revelation of God, images of God, and the Eucharist? The following are some starter ideas for you:

- Discuss the Scriptures. For example, look up Luke, chapter 15, and talk about the images of God as housewife, as shepherd, and as forgiving father. Discuss your faith in a God who will do anything to search for us, find us, and show love for us.
- Discuss the story at the beginning of this chapter. What were you thinking and feeling as you read it? If you had been in the chat room, what would you have said? What nickname would you have given yourself? Which chat room friend did you most relate to? Which did you least relate to?
- Take a look at a difficult issue: All over the world, even in this country, women are often discriminated against. They are half the population, and yet they do not have half the voice. While women do an equal share of the work of the world, men earn most of the money. In some countries, women do not have any rights at all. Husbands are allowed to beat and rape their wives. Think about how our language at Mass and other prayer experiences might support the notion that males are superior to females.
- Be a friend. Remember that every person, female or male, has value, worth, and significance. Understand that females can make males uncomfortable, and males can make females uncomfortable. Be open to those possibilities, and be ready to discuss them without being judgmental.
- Let the symbols speak. Pay attention to the way people speak of God. Hear how often a masculine pronoun is used, even at Mass. Consider

the qualities of God. Notice that they are qualities seen in both males and females. Be more open to the way you image God. Let a new image enrich your prayer life.

- Note the reason for the season. Certain holy days encourage us to focus on our image of God. The feast of Trinity Sunday and the feast of the body and blood of Christ occur on the two Sundays that follow Pentecost Sunday. All three feasts focus on an image of God. Saint Patrick's Day and the feast of the baptism of the Lord are feast days that call us to focus on one God in three persons.

Take Time to Pray

This prayer works well when teenagers and parents pray it together. It can also work with one person alone or with a small group of friends.

THE CALL TO PRAYER

Light a candle with three wicks, or light three candles, while addressing God as Trinity. Use a title for God you don't often hear, such as one of the titles in the following prayer:

In the name of the Almighty, the Eternal Word, and the Divine Spirit, amen.

GOD'S WORD

Read 2 Cor 13.11–13.

REFLECTION

You pray to a God who has been adored and worshiped by many men and women throughout history. So much mystery, so little understanding, so much faith. Yet so simple a message: Live in peace. Greet one another with a holy kiss. Put things in order. Know that God is with you. Know that the grace of Jesus, the love of the Almighty, and the communion of the Spirit bless you. Do you know that? Do you feel it in your bones? Do you embrace it with every fiber in your being? Do you hear God calling your name? Are you ready to answer?

BLESSING

Lift up your hands and cup them near the three flames. Feel the heat. Ask for the blessing from the Triune God upon yourself, your friends, and your family.

The Pastoral Circle

Awareness is the stage at which a person becomes conscious of an injustice. It may come directly through personal experience if a person is exposed to an injustice first-hand. Often, however, awareness comes from some other source—through a personal witness, a written account, a simulation activity, or some other means.

Analysis is the stage at which we begin to move past simply being conscious of an injustice and try to understand why the injustice occurred. We try to search the political, social, economic, and cultural factors that relate to the problem, in order to work toward a solution.

Reflection is the stage at which we interface our personal values and our faith with the analysis of the injustice. In this stage we search our faith traditions, the Scriptures, our Catholic social teaching, and the lived faith of our church community.

Action is the stage at which we follow a direct course of active response to an injustice. Complex social issues are seldom resolved with simple solutions, and the action stage rarely solves the problem of the injustice. The action stage often leads to further awareness, however, which in turn leads to more analysis and reflection.

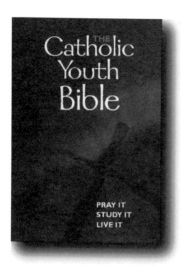

The Catholic Youth Bible

PRAY IT STUDY IT LIVE IT

NEW REVISED STANDARD VERSION: CATHOLIC EDITION

BRIAN SINGER-TOWNS, GENERAL EDITOR

Over 650 lively articles draw on the most current biblical scholarship to address the interests and real-life concerns of today's young people.

ISBN 0-88489-489-4, paper, $27.95
ISBN 0-88489-667-6, hardcover, $37.95

We Are Fire!

COMPANION SONGS
FOR *THE CATHOLIC YOUTH BIBLE*

Some of the world's finest Christian musicians sing songs that reflect one of six biblical themes. Artists include David Kauffman, Scarecrow & Tinmen, David Haas, Steve Angrisano, Jesse Manibusan, and more!

ISBN 0-88489-645-5, compact disc, 55 minutes $15.95

Ask for *The Catholic Youth Bible* at your favorite bookstore, or call 800-533-8095, or visit the Saint Mary's Press web site at **www.smp.org**.

SAINT MARY'S PRESS
702 TERRACE HEIGHTS
WINONA, MN 55987-1320